Child Care
and
the ADA

Child Care and the ADA

A Handbook for Inclusive Programs

by

Victoria Youcha Rab, Ed.D.
Project Director
Community Connections Project
The George Washington University
Washington, D.C.

and

Karren Ikeda Wood, Ed.S.
Training Coordinator
Community Connections Project
The George Washington University
Washington, D.C.

with a special contribution by

Janeen McCracken Taylor, Ph.D.
Assistant Professor
Department of Special Education
Division of Education
School of Continuing Studies
The Johns Hopkins University
Baltimore

·P·A·U·L·H·
BROOKES
PUBLISHING C°

Baltimore • London • Toronto • Sydney

Paul H. Brookes Publishing Co.
Post Office Box 10624
Baltimore, Maryland 21285-0624

Typeset by Brushwood Graphics, Inc., Baltimore, Maryland.
Manufactured in the United States of America by
The Maple Press Company, York, Pennsylvania.

The information in this book is not a substitute for legal advice. If you need specific legal information about how PL 101-336, the Americans with Disabilities Act (ADA) of 1990, applies to you, seek the assistance of a lawyer who is familiar with the ADA requirements.

Library of Congress Cataloging-in-Publication Data

Rab, Victoria Youcha.
    Child care and the ADA : a handbook for inclusive programs /
Victoria Youcha Rab & Karren Ikeda Wood and a special contribution
from Janeen Taylor.
        p.   cm.
        Includes bibliographical references and index.
        ISBN 1-55766-185-5
        1. Day care centers—Law and legislation—United States.   2. Child care services—Law
and legislation—United States.   3. Discrimination against the handicapped—Law and
legislation—United States.   4. Handicapped children—Legal status, laws, etc.—United
States.   I. Wood, Karren Ikeda.   II. Taylor, Janeen McCracken, 1946–   .   III. Title.
KF2042.D3R33   1995
344.73′032712—dc20
[347.30432712]   95-1056
                                                                                                              CIP

British Library Cataloguing-in-Publication data are available from the British Library.

CONTENTS

ABOUT THE AUTHORS

Victoria Youcha Rab, Ed.D., is Project Director of the Community Connections Project, The George Washington University, School of Education and Human Development, Department of Teacher Preparation and Special Education, Washington, D.C. As director, she works to prepare child care professionals to include children with disabilities. Dr. Rab has worked with young children and their families in a variety of capacities since 1975. She has been a preschool special education teacher, director of a program for infants with disabilities and their families, a child development specialist in a pediatric practice, and the coordinator of federally funded training projects for early childhood personnel.

Karren Ikeda Wood, Ed.S., O.T.R., is Training Coordinator of the Community Connections Project, and Co-director of the Master's Training Project in Traumatic Brain Injury, School of Education and Human Development, Department of Teacher Preparation and Special Education, The George Washington University, Washington, D.C. In most recent years, she has promoted and supported efforts to include children with disabilities in child care programs. Previously she provided occupational therapy services for individuals with developmental disabilities, directed an early intervention program, and administered programs for children and adults with developmental disabilities and autism.

Janeen McCracken Taylor, Ph.D., is Assistant Professor for the Department of Special Education, Division of Education, School of Continuing Studies, The Johns Hopkins University, Baltimore, where she teaches graduate courses and directs personnel preparations initiatives. Dr. Taylor earned her doctorate at the University of New Mexico and then served as the early childhood specialist for the Maryland State Department of Education (MSDE). During her time at MSDE, she was closely involved in policy development–related communicable diseases in educational settings and special health care needs of children with disabilities. For the past several years, Dr. Taylor has focused on the preparation of early intervention and early childhood special education teachers.

FOREWORD

Child Care and the ADA: A Handbook for Inclusive Programs is tailor made for program directors and child care personnel who have been puzzled, bewildered, and just plain worried about what new federal guidelines will mean for their daily practices and procedures when children with disabilities are admitted to their programs. This handbook arrives like the proverbial knight in shining armor in order to rescue programs distressed by the unknown—how to develop the skills and knowledge to enrich the lives of young children who exhibit one or a variety of physical, emotional, cognitive, linguistic, and motor difficulties and how to meet the needs of their families.

Part I of this book begins systematically with definitions of federal laws, such as PL 101-336, the Americans with Disabilities Act (ADA) of 1990, and PL 101-476, the Individuals with Disabilities Education Act (IDEA) of 1990, and what they mandate in terms of provisions for serving children with disabilities. Obligations, rights, and responsibilities are clearly spelled out.

Part II serves as a guide for administrators who want to make inclusion work successfully in their programs. Step by encouraging step, the authors lead program directors and staff into the world of expanding service that will include serving children with disabilities. Filled with rich, vivid vignettes that reflect real-world problems and issues that child care staff will face, this book guides the reader clearly through the process from initial telephone contacts, and later face-to-face interactions with parents, to the daily interactions and dialogues that serve to create a supportive environment for the child.

Part III zeroes in on real-life situations and problems that staff will have to grapple with in implementing an inclusive program for preschoolers. This section is both lucid and complete in providing information, ideas about what works, how-to techniques, and examples of appropriate and inappropriate program practices. It will enable child care facilities to gain cognitive control over the ideas and processes involved in planning to adhere to and then meeting federal guidelines. Administrators will have a strong friend in this handbook, a friend who will help them provide quality service to include children with disabilities in their programs.

The handbook not only gives information and advice; it is also profoundly democratic in addressing inclusion issues. Inclusion is not to be dictated from the top down. Instead, an administrator is guided forthrightly to examine the importance of involving all staff in preparation for efforts to become an inclusive program. Good suggestions are given for methods by which the director can systematically involve staff in careful preparations for accepting children with disabilities. The authors give pragmatically feasible ideas on how to retrain staff, how to modify facilities, as well as how to identify and mobilize community resources that can support the adventure of carrying out an inclusive program.

Careful and extensive discussions of many practical topics such as access to the physical space, opportunities for maximizing learning, usability of equipment, room arrangements, schedules, and curricular issues make this volume particularly useful in the planning stages of participating in work toward developing an inclusive program. These discussions will be helpful in enlightening administrators about what kinds of changes may be necessary in order to provide optimal service. The importance of sharpening adult observation skills and being flexible is eloquently emphasized. Such enhancement of teacher skills should benefit all children in programs, not just children with disabilities.

Innovative suggestions are made, such as encouraging teamwork among teachers and the formation of buddy systems between typical youngsters and their peers with disabilities. Breaking tasks down into components and planning activities that meet multiple, rather than single, learning goals are among the wise suggestions elaborated.

Trouble-shooting low-cost solutions to problems of access are given. For example, suppose the youngster does not have a motor disability, but the parent does. The parent must use a wheelchair and cannot deliver the child to his or her preschool classroom. Simple solutions, such as designating a staff person to meet the parent as he or she drives up at arrival time in the morning and to help the child climb the stairs to the classroom, are suggested and encouraged when a facility cannot afford to build a wheelchair-accessible ramp.

The authors are particularly sensitive to the possible past history of discouragement and rejection that both a child with a disability and his or her family have faced in trying to find appropriate inclusive placement. The emphasis on encouraging staff empathy for each child and for parents, as well as encouraging peer empathy and prosocial interactions with a child with a disability, will broaden the programmatic framework of caregivers who have perhaps concentrated more on cognitive goals than on prosocial goals in their classrooms. Role playing that incorporates, for example, the use of a wheelchair or the use of earmuffs (to simulate the sound environment for a child with a hearing disability) are suggested as techniques to encourage peer understanding and empathy.

The handbook explains clearly that sometimes difficult issues and stresses will arise as inclusion is practiced. Detailed descriptions of special services that a child may need after evaluation and preparation of the individualized education program (IEP) and individualized family service plan (IFSP) for each child and family are included.

Janeen McCracken Taylor has prepared the concluding chapter to this handbook. She addresses questions of health and health-maintenance procedures in a program for young children. This chapter will be useful for staff training on procedures for prevention of infections in any facility. Some children with disabilities, such as children with cystic fibrosis, are particularly vulnerable to infections. The hand-washing prescriptions and other techniques counseled in this final chapter will be important for staff to learn about whether or not they have a child with a disability in the classroom.

Constantly throughout this book, the authors pose Socratic questions for the reader. These questions will galvanize administrators and staff to keep on thinking and creating workable solutions to problems they may encounter in fully implementing an inclusive program. The wisdom of the authors' guidance comes through clearly as they write, "A child with a disability is a child first and shares the same feelings, needs, and interests as typical children. This child also has some needs that are different from those of typical children. . . . learning about who the child is and what he or she needs must go beyond a label or diagnosis"(p. 125).

Thus, this handbook, by helping administrators and caregivers meet the needs of children with disabilities, is actually setting the stage for *individualization* of the program for every child served. Caregivers who learn how to adjust strategies and learning activities to accommodate a variety of learning styles and abilities will be increasing their competence to optimize the learning experiences and socialization successes of all children in the program.

With good will, hard work, perseverance, and the practical, helpful guidance of this handbook, a child care facility, together with the parents and supportive community specialists, can embark on the adventure of truly serving all young children well—whatever their individual needs may be.

Alice Sterling Honig, Ph.D.
Professor of Child Development
Syracuse University
Syracuse, New York

FOREWORD

The inclusion of children with varying abilities has the potential to improve early child care and education for all children because it focuses our attention on the individuality of each child. This does not mean that running a good inclusive program is easy. There are additional rules and regulations to follow, funding implications to deal with, prejudices and misconceptions to confront, new information on development to learn, program modifications to consider, and community resources to explore. But the essentials for making inclusion work—a functional environment, parent involvement, and a developmentally appropriate curriculum—are present in all programs that are doing a good job with the children and families currently enrolled.

In *Child Care and the ADA: A Handbook for Inclusive Programs,* Victoria Rab and Karren Wood offer the additional information needed by early childhood educators to initiate inclusion and make it work. They provide, in clear and practical terms, the information and support needed by early child care programs to make the necessary modifications in their policies and practices. Implementing the suggestions in this book can make the difference between success and disappointment for programs that want to do a good job of including children with varying abilities. Administrators and teaching staff will find their examples and anecdotes particularly helpful in personalizing, humanizing, and demystifying inclusion.

As early childhood educators, we are the people closest to parents as they raise their children. We are in a position to share information and offer parents our warm support in their most important role. Inclusive programs challenge us to broaden our perspectives and sharpen our skills so that we can serve each child and family more fully. The information in this book will help programs create the conditions that make effective relationships between staff and families possible. Then these caring adults can work together to improve the lives of children.

Thelma Harms, Ph.D.
Frank Porter Graham Child Development Center
University of North Carolina at Chapel Hill
Chapel Hill, North Carolina

PREFACE

This book was written to guide child care professionals in their efforts to include children with disabilities. We have worked for many years to bring children with disabilities into community settings and have come to know and appreciate the efforts that are made on behalf of the children and families served at quality child care centers.

The passage of PL 101-336, the Americans with Disabilities Act (ADA) of 1990, has highlighted the issue of serving children with disabilities in child care settings. However, understanding the law is only the beginning. We hope that children with disabilities will be welcomed into child care programs. The information in this book is intended to support those efforts.

We strongly believe that even without the benefit of federal legislation, *all* children have the right to belong and be active participants in their communities. Furthermore, we believe that child care settings can be wonderful places for children with and without disabilities to begin their educational journeys together.

ACKNOWLEDGMENTS

Many thanks to our colleagues, especially Dr. Maxine Freund, who reviewed and edited the early versions of this book. We are also grateful to Abby Cohen and Kristi Bleyer for their legal guidance and our editor, Victoria Thulman, who patiently shaped this book into its present form. We offer a special thanks to Janeen McCracken Taylor, who contributed the chapter, "Staying Healthy." Finally, we thank our families, especially our in-house editors Geraldine Youcha and David Ikeda.

To the many
child care professionals, children, and families
whose experiences have made this book
come to life

Child Care
and
the ADA

I

How Do Disability Laws Affect Your Child Care Program?

Part I of this book explains how PL 101-336, the Americans with Disabilities Act (ADA) of 1990, applies to child care settings. In addition to the ADA, other federal disability laws are included to illustrate how laws are interrelated and to guide child care professionals in finding appropriate services for the children in their care.

1

The Americans with Disabilities Act

Child Care as a Public Accommodation

PL 101-336, the Americans with Disabilities Act (ADA) of 1990, grew from Section 504 of the Rehabilitation Act of 1973, PL 93-112, and Titles VI and VII of the Civil Rights Act of 1964, PL 102-166. Title VI extended protection against discrimination of people because of race, color, or national origin in programs and activities that receive federal financial assistance. Title VII extended protection against discrimination of people because of race, color, religion, gender, or national origin in employment. The ADA makes illegal discrimination against Americans of all ages who have disabilities and their families.

> It is the purpose of this act (1) to provide a clear and comprehensive national mandate for the elimination of discrimination against individuals with disabilities . . . (4) to involve the sweep of congressional authority, . . . in order to address the major areas of discrimination faced day-to-day by people with disabilities. (PL 101-336, Section 2[b])

When Congress passed the ADA in 1990, it cited the fact that some 43,000,000 Americans had physical or mental disabilities. Historically, society has segregated and isolated these individuals. Legislation was necessary to end that discrimination.

The Americans with Disabilities Act is largely based on Section 504, but broadens this coverage to include most private and state facilities that do business with the public even if they receive no federal funds. The ADA sends a clear message to the American people that those with disabilities are entitled to the same rights and privileges as others enjoy. The ADA guarantees equal opportunity to qualified individuals with disabilities

- To obtain employment based on abilities
- To receive services provided by state or local governments

- To have access to public accommodations (e.g., facilities that provide lodging; food; retail goods; medical, educational, and recreational services)
- To obtain private and public transportation
- To have the opportunity to use telecommunications

The act is made up of five titles.

Title I—Employment
Title II—Public Services, including Transportation
Title III—Public Accommodations
Title IV—Telecommunications
Title V—Miscellaneous Provisions

Of these five titles, Title I, Employment, and Title III, Public Accommodations, have the biggest impact on private child care settings. This chapter explains how Title III applies to private child care centers, and Chapter 2 provides more detail about how Title I applies.

How will the provisions of the ADA affect your center? What parts of the law will have the most impact on your program? This section of the chapter presents an overview of the ADA, explains the language of the law, and describes the specific requirements that apply to early childhood settings.

The information in this chapter is not a substitute for legal advice. If you need specific legal information about how the ADA applies to you, seek the assistance of a lawyer who is familiar with ADA requirements.

TO WHOM DOES THE LAW APPLY?

Title III of the ADA applies to private early childhood programs and the children and families they serve when an individual with a disability is involved. If your center is run by a state or local government entity, you are covered by Title II of the ADA, Public Services, and will need to meet somewhat different requirements. Consult the Title II regulations to determine your specific obligations.

Title III of the law defines an *individual with a disability* in the following way:

> with respect to an individual, a physical or mental impairment that substantially limits one or more major life activities of such individual; a record of such an impairment or being regarded as having an impairment. (PL 101-336, Section 3 [2])

Major life activities include the following:

- Caring for oneself
- Performing manual tasks
- Walking
- Seeing
- Hearing

- Speaking
- Breathing
- Learning
- Working

In addition to people who are limited substantially in one or more major life activities, the law covers people in three other categories. First, it protects those who are regarded as having an impairment even though they are not limited in any major life activity. A child with a disfiguring facial burn who is not limited in any major life activity would qualify under this definition because he or she might experience discrimination because of his or her appearance.

Second, this definition covers people who have a history of having an impairment. Children with a history of leukemia or heart defects may not be acutely ill or limited in any significant way, but are covered by this definition because they could be discriminated against on the basis of their medical status.

Some of the conditions specifically protected by the law include cancer, human immunodeficiency virus (HIV), hepatitis B, and noncontagious tuberculosis. Again, the law protects people with these conditions if they are substantially limited in one or more major life activities or if they have a history of having such a condition. The listing is not exhaustive, and people with other medical conditions also may be entitled to protection.

Third, a separate section of the ADA also prohibits discrimination when a person is associated with an individual with a disability. This association may be a family relationship, a friendship, or a business association. For example, a child could not be denied admission to a child care center because his or her parent or sibling has a disability. Alternatively, a child could not be denied admission to a child care program because one of his or her friends is known to have HIV.

WHO MUST COMPLY WITH THE LAW?

Early childhood facilities are part of the definition of public accommodations under Title III of the ADA. Hotels, restaurants, stores, museums, parks, and movie theaters are also examples of public accommodations.

> A facility, operated by a private entity, whose operations affect commerce and fall within at least one of the following categories . . .
>
> (J)   A *nursery*, elementary, secondary, undergraduate, or postgraduate private school, or *other place of education*;
>
> (K)   A *day care center*, senior citizen center, or other social service center establishment (PL 101-336, Title III, Section 301 [2])

Title III of the ADA contains a broad exemption for religious institutions and entities. Nursery schools and child care centers operated by churches are not subject to the requirements of the law.

The deciding factor for exemption is whether the religious institution or an independent group controls the operation and finances of the center. If a church rents space to an independent day care center, that center is covered by the law. However, if a church donates space to a child care center, that center may be exempt from the law. Money must be paid for the law to apply.

Even though schools and centers run by religious institutions may be exempt from Title III of the ADA, other federal and state nondiscrimination laws may apply. Religious entities, for example, must still comply with Title I (Employment) with some modifications. Programs should check with their licensing division and State Attorney General's Office to find out what other requirements apply to them.

WHAT KINDS OF CHANGES DOES THE LAW REQUIRE?

Child care centers must have programs that are as physically accessible as possible and modifications must be made in the policies, practices, and procedures to ensure that discrimination does not occur against people with disabilities. The requirements of the law are closely tied to the resources of the individual center and will vary from center to center. Centers must assess the potential for change or modification and decide on a case-by-case basis which changes are realistic, both financially and logistically, at the present time.

Removing Physical Barriers

> Readily achievable means easily accomplished and able to be carried out without much difficulty or expense. (PL 101-336, Title III, Section 301)

The standard in the law for deciding what centers are required to do to make their facilities physically accessible is the term *readily achievable*. Centers must remove physical barriers and make architectural changes that can be carried out without much difficulty or expense. As stated earlier, each center must carefully consider the requirements of the law and determine the feasibility of making changes on a case-by-case basis. A small center may be able to change door knobs but not install a ramp or may be able to modify an existing bathroom. What is readily achievable for a large corporate child care center might be unrealistic for a small neighborhood center.

Factors that the law considers when deciding if removal of a physical barrier is readily achievable include

- The nature and cost of the action
- The overall financial resources of the site or sites involved
- Legitimate safety requirements necessary for safe operation

- The overall financial resources of any parent corporation or entity, if applicable

The following example shows the kind of changes that might be needed to comply with the law and how a large center approached renovations. For a more detailed discussion of program changes see Part II, Chapter 5.

◄o► ◄o► ◄o►

Kiddie Country III is part of a chain of national child care centers. The center serves 150 children ages 6 months to 5 years. The facility was built in the 1980s and although it is all on one level, it is not fully accessible because of curbs, steps into the building, small bathroom stalls, heavy doors, door knobs, and a security pass card system at eye level.

Before the ADA went into effect, Kiddie Country's central business office assigned a program administrator to look at compliance issues and make recommendations to all of its site directors. All of the Kiddie Country centers conducted studies of their physical accessibility using surveys developed by the program administrator who had consulted an architect about the accessibility guidelines. Each site director documented areas that were out of compliance with the law. The central office then established priorities for changes.

For Kiddie Country III this meant adding curb cuts and a ramp at the front door for wheelchair access to the building, widening a bathroom stall and adding handrails, changing the doorknobs to make them easier to open, and enlarging the reception area to make it easier for a person in a wheelchair to maneuver.

These changes were expensive and the center had to raise tuition rates to help offset the costs (see Tuition Rates in this chapter). The central office allocated money for additional changes in the coming years to allow all the centers to alter playgrounds and classrooms gradually. As a for-profit chain they took advantage of the available tax credits and deductions allowed by the ADA.

◄o► ◄o► ◄o►

All programs for young children are expected to make readily achievable changes to physically accommodate those with disabilities. These include making existing facilities readily accessible and usable. Changes do not have to be expensive always. Examples of simple, low-cost changes include the following:

- Screening off part of a bathroom to provide privacy for the diapering of older children
- Installing wooden ramps
- Using labels that can be identified by touch so a child with a visual impairment can use materials independently
- Lowering coat hooks for a child in a wheelchair

In one nursery school, the children helped to make accommodations for one of their classmates.

◀○▶ ◀○▶ ◀○▶

Dion, who has a short-stature syndrome (i.e., achondroplasia), had just started in the 4-year-old class and it took the other children a few days to notice that he was shorter than everyone else. Finally, Maria said to the teacher, "Dion can't reach the sink." The teacher asked the children what they could do so Dion could reach things. After a lively discussion, Dion and the others decided to use the big wooden blocks to build a platform next to the sink. Then someone found a milk crate by Dion's cubby so he could reach the coat hook. The teacher made certain that the platform and milk crate could support Dion safely. There already was a step stool in the bathroom, so that was not a problem.

◀○▶ ◀○▶ ◀○▶

By allowing the children to help decide on the changes, the teacher communicated that everyone belonged and that they were responsible for helping each other. The children noticed that Dion was different, but his differences did not set him apart and the changes did not take a lot of time or cost a lot of money.

Alternatives to Barrier Removal

If it is not possible to remove a barrier, programs must investigate other ways to make their facility accessible. If a classroom is on the second floor and the parent of a child in the class is in a wheelchair, a staff person could meet the child at the car. Similarly, if the bathroom in the classroom is not wheelchair accessible, but there is an accessible bathroom in another location, the teacher could accompany a child in a wheelchair to that bathroom.

One mother told this story about her efforts to have her daughter attend her neighborhood preschool. Kim is 4 years old, has cerebral palsy, and uses a wheelchair.

◀○▶ ◀○▶ ◀○▶

Our county is promoting the policy of inclusion and our daughter Kim participates in an inclusive preschool classroom. She rides the bus across town to another school so she can go to class with children her age who are not disabled. She could have gone to a preschool in our neighborhood, but the 4-year-old groups are on the second floor and there is no elevator. If just one 4-year-old group could be moved to the ground floor, Kim would be fine, but we haven't been able to get the preschool's board of directors to consider that possibility.

◀○▶ ◀○▶ ◀○▶

Because of the ADA, Kim's mother has the right to approach the administrators at her neighborhood preschool and ask them to reconsider. Moving a classroom to another floor might well be considered a reasonable alternative to the prohibitive cost of installing an elevator.

A Continuing Obligation for Compliance

The ADA requires child care centers to continually assess the changes they can make to become as physically accessible as possible. No center is required to exceed the requirements of the law but centers are required to continue to make efforts to comply with the legal standards.

In the example of Kiddie Country, the center studied its level of physical accessibility and began the process of barrier removal and architectural changes. The staff decided what changes were readily achievable at the present time and made plans for future changes. If Kiddie Country found that it could not afford to make some changes this year, then it would have to reevaluate its position in the future to see if the changes would be more affordable at a later date or if new alternatives have become available.

New Construction

With few exceptions, all new construction and alterations to existing facilities must be readily accessible and usable by people with disabilities to the extent that it is not structurally impracticable. Centers should follow the Americans with Disabilities Act Accessibility Guidelines (ADAAG), issued by the Architectural and Transportation Barriers Compliance Board. Chapter 5, in this book, discusses some of these specific requirements. Check with your architect or building contractor to be sure any new construction or alterations to your center will meet these standards.

Modifications in Policies, Practices, and Procedures

Child care centers must make changes in their admissions policies, enrollment procedures, and daily practices to accommodate children and adults with disabilities.

The ADA requires these changes unless a modification would *fundamentally alter the nature* of the services the center provides.

Admissions Policies   The ADA prohibits the

> imposition or application of eligibility criteria that screen out or tend to screen out an individual with a disability . . . from fully and equally enjoying any goods, services, facilities, advantages, and accommodations, unless such criteria can be shown to be necessary for the provision of the goods, services, facilities, privileges, advantages, or accommodations being offered. (PL 101-336, Title III, Section 302 [2][A][i])

This requirement means that the admissions policies and enrollment procedures of early childhood programs should not intentionally or unintentionally exclude children with disabilities.

The one circumstance under which a program may have a restrictive policy is when a specific admission criterion is *fundamental to the nature of the services being offered*. For example, a school for children with musical gifts might require an audition to show that the applicant can sing in key and might reject any applicant who could not pass this test. If the school did not have this requirement, it would substantially change the type of program it offered. Therefore, this restrictive admissions requirement probably would be allowed under the ADA. However, this exemption will not apply to most programs for young children.

Many centers expect that all children in the 2-year-old group would be walking. Because walking is not fundamental to the nature of the services being offered, as a requirement for admission, this policy could discriminate against children with physical disabilities.

Another common expectation of many early childhood facilities is that children be toilet trained before admission. Because this criterion applies to all children it appears at first to be nondiscriminatory. But the toilet training requirement screens out a group of children with disabilities, among them children with spina bifida who lack bowel and bladder control. Therefore, it might be considered a violation of the law.

One section (Sec. 36.306) of the ADA regulations says that services of a personal nature; which include eating, dressing, and toileting; do not have to be provided unless they are a service generally provided by the facility. If a center changes diapers or provides toileting assistance to any group, they probably need to provide the same service to all children with disabilities. But if they do not diaper any child and enroll only school-age children who ordinarily do not require toileting assistance, the admissions requirement of toilet training might stand. In situations like this, when the law is unclear, you may ask for guidance directly from the federal Department of Justice. The appropriate telephone numbers are listed in the Resources at the end of this book. Clearly the ADA was not written with diapering in mind and it may well have to be decided by a case in court.

◄○► ◄○► ◄○►

Mrs. Smythe tried to enroll her son Connor in a child care center near her job. Connor, who has spina bifida, was 4 years old at the time. He walks with crutches and he will never have good bowel and bladder control because of his disability. He was denied admission because he wasn't toilet trained. The child care center said that its policy required that all children be toilet trained by age 3 and that the teachers in the 4-year-old class didn't change diapers. The teachers informed Mrs. Smythe that they were sorry but Connor could not enroll.

◄○► ◄○► ◄○►

Under the ADA, this policy would be considered discriminatory. Because the teachers help other children when they have a toileting accident by cleaning up the child and changing wet clothes, the teachers would be capable of helping Connor. Connor's needs are not dramatically different. Although the teachers in the 4-year-old class may not like changing an older child's diapers, this should not interfere with Connor's right to attend.

The best approach in such circumstances is to work with the family and make adaptations where feasible. For example, a staff person could be assigned to assist an older child with toileting, or part of a regular bathroom could be screened off to provide privacy for diapering. An extra change of clothes could be kept on hand for both the staff person and the child, and a complete changing kit could be assembled in advance. Community resources such as the local chapter of The Arc (formerly the Association for Retarded Citizens of the United States) or special education staff from the public schools are often available to provide free or low cost in-service training on diapering and toileting assistance for older children. These arrangements probably would not be too disruptive, time consuming, or expensive, nor would they *fundamentally alter the nature of the services provided*, so the center would likely be expected to make the adaptations.

Enrollment Forms   Given that most children with disabilities will be allowed in your program under the ADA, it would be wise to review your enrollment forms to be sure your criteria are not discriminatory. Your enrollment forms may not include questions about the presence of a disability because the law says you may not unnecessarily inquire about the presence of a disability. You are allowed to ask only for information that is necessary for the safe operation of your program. It is appropriate to ask about specific skills or developmental milestones if the same information is collected on all children. The form used for admission to the program should not request any information that possibly could be used in a discriminatory way. After admission, a second form could be used to collect additional medical information and could include optional questions that relate to any special needs. Parents should be given a choice about whether to disclose that their child has a disability. The form should make it clear that any information the parents choose to disclose will be used to make appropriate program decisions and adaptations, and will not be used for discriminatory purposes.

Tuition Rates

The ADA also addresses tuition rates. Programs may not charge a higher tuition rate for children with disabilities. Costs incurred in complying with the act may not be passed on to the family of the child with the disability only. Instead, programs may raise tuition for all children to cover increased costs. In an earlier example about removal of physical barriers, Kiddie Country chose to raise tuition to cover some of its alteration expenses. Because children with disabilities require the same things that quality programs provide for all children—developmentally appropriate group size and ratios, safe and enticing toys and materials, and knowledgeable and caring staff—raising tuition rates is rarely necessary when modifying program practices. If a child with a disability requires "extra" services such as speech-language therapy, the program is allowed to charge the individual family for that service because it is over and above what the program typically provides and what the ADA requires. However, programs may not charge the family of a student for the costs of installing a ramp or buying books in braille. Those costs are related to the program and, therefore, are accommodations required by the law.

WHAT ARE AUXILIARY AIDS AND SERVICES?

Auxiliary aids and services are the things people with speech, learning, hearing, or visual impairments need to communicate effectively. They include the following:

- Sign language interpreters
- Written materials and assistive listening devices
- Note takers
- Readers
- Taped texts
- Braille or large print materials

Any person with a disability that compromises communication may need auxiliary aids and services.

Child care centers must provide auxiliary aids and services unless doing so would fundamentally alter the nature of their program or would impose an undue burden. The definition of *undue burden* is identical to the definition of *undue hardship* used in Title I of the ADA as the limitation on an employer's obligation to reasonably accommodate an applicant or employee. Under both limitations, child care centers do not have to do things that involve "significant difficulty or expense." However, the undue burden standard that applies to the provision of auxiliary aids and services requires a greater level of effort than does the "readily available" standard for removing physical barriers in existing facilities. Even though the standards are different, the factors to be considered in determining what qualifies as an undue burden are identical to those listed previously for determining what is readily achievable.

The ADA requires that programs have the capacity to communicate with people with disabilities. However, child care centers may choose how they wish to provide effective communication for their employees, families, and children with disabilities. The method should be selected in conjunction with the people it is designed to serve. For example, if a mother has a visual impairment, she and the center staff may agree that all announcements will be read to her when she picks up her daughter.

In another case, if a child is deaf and communicates using sign language, his or her teacher could take a sign language course. When field trips and special programs are arranged, it would be important to ask if a sign language interpreter is available or seek a volunteer who signs.

If a center needs to communicate with parents who have hearing impairments, a special Telecommunications Device for the Deaf (TDD) can be purchased. A TDD sends and receives messages in print when attached to a telephone line. If the expense of a TDD is too great, the center could use a relay service instead. With a relay service the caller dials a special operator who then transmits the message to or from the person with the hearing impairment. Every state now has a free relay service. Call your local telephone company to find out how to access this service in your community.

WHAT IF MY PROGRAM PROVIDES TRANSPORTATION?

If an early childhood program provides transportation, it must make arrangements to provide the same level of transportation to all children. If the center offers daily transportation to and from home, it must offer this service to any child with a disability. This might mean using a special car seat or removing a seat in a van and adding "tie-downs" (straps that secure a wheelchair) to accommodate a wheelchair.

The transportation standard in the law is the same as that for barrier removal in existing facilities. Child care centers are expected to remove transportation barriers to the extent that it is "readily achievable" to do so. For the most part, centers are not required to buy new vehicles or install lifts, but they must remove whatever barriers they can so that transportation is accessible. The major exception is if a center provides regular transportation in vehicles that hold 16 or more people. In this case, vehicles purchased or leased after August 26, 1990, must be "readily accessible to and usable by individuals with disabilities, including those who use wheelchairs" (PL 101-336, Title III, Section 302).

If a program regularly does not provide transportation, but goes on field trips with parent drivers, the program must make efforts to provide appropriate transportation so the child with a disability can participate.

IS IT EVER PERMISSIBLE TO EXCLUDE A CHILD?

Direct threat means a significant risk to the health or safety of others that cannot be eliminated by a modification of policies, practices, or procedures or by the provision of auxiliary aids or services. (PL 101-336, Title III, Section 302)

The law specifies one special situation where early childhood programs may deny services to people with disabilities. Programs are not expected to include individuals who pose a direct threat to the health and safety of children or staff.

This situation concerns the rare instance in which the presence of a child or family member with a disability might pose a risk to others. Programs must make the determination of direct threat on an individual basis after conducting an individual assessment based on reasonable judgment, current medical evidence, and/or the best available objective evidence. The nature, duration, and severity of the risk must be documented as well as the probability that the potential injury will actually occur. In addition, the program must indicate whether reasonable modifications of policies, practices, or procedures will mitigate the risk. In order for a child to be considered a direct threat, a program must prove three criteria:

1. The program has tried to make changes and accommodations.
2. The changes and accommodations were unsuccessful.
3. The child is likely to cause or continue to cause significant harm to other children and/or staff.

Programs should document how often any unusual behavior occurs, the circumstances under which the behavior occurs, and any steps taken by the staff to deal with the behavior. It is important to keep written records of all efforts to deal with the problem and changes that have taken place. Such records may be needed as evidence if the determination of direct threat is challenged.

The following example illustrates the complexity of establishing direct threat. A 2-year-old who has bitten another child several times probably does not qualify as a direct threat, because biting is not developmentally unusual for a 2-year-old child. However, an older child with a disability who bites, hits, or is otherwise aggressive to staff and children might be covered under this provision.

When Mrs. Samuels enrolled her 3-year-old son Derek in a full-day program, the director soon felt that Derek posed a direct threat to the other children.

◄◦► ◄◦► ◄◦►

Derek had attended Blue Bird Preschool only 3 weeks when I had the unhappy task of calling Mrs. Samuels to tell her that she must look for another program for her son. Derek was biting other children at least once a day and the school policy is to suspend any child who has bitten another child twice in 1 week. I reviewed in my mind all the accommodations that the program had made. We took him even though he has autism. We put him in with the younger kids so he would be with children closer to his developmental level and we've read his individualized education program and talked with his special education teacher. We've been very patient with Derek. How could anyone expect us to do more? Some of the other parents were very upset. I was afraid I would lose some of the other families and I felt I couldn't afford that.

Mrs. Samuels tried to change my mind. She explained again that because Derek can't talk, this is the only way he can defend himself when other children try to take his toys. She also explained that when he gets excited, he bites. He is not trying to be mean or hurt others. Derek had made so much progress in the 3 weeks he'd been in school. He'd learned the routine, how to play with the toys, and he even started to pay attention to the other children.

◄○► ◄○► ◄○►

This is a difficult situation for everyone. The center has tried several approaches to manage Derek's biting behavior, yet they have been unsuccessful. The director is understandably concerned for the other children and the families in the program. Nevertheless, the ADA requires that programs look extensively for outside assistance from community agencies and document their efforts before making a determination of direct threat.

The director could call her public school or developmental disabilities agency to see if they have a behavioral specialist who could observe Derek and develop a plan to manage his behavior. She could talk again with Derek's special education teacher and ask what other supports for children with autism are available. Placing Derek with younger children might seem appropriate for his developmental level, but his behavior might not be such a problem if he were with children closer to his own age. His peers might be better able to defend themselves against Derek's biting attempts. Finally, 3 weeks may not be enough time for Derek to adjust and learn the routine. The director must decide how much of a threat Derek's biting poses to the other children. Pressure from other parents should not influence her decision.

Child care centers may sometimes find themselves in a position of denying admission to a child for another reason. The general requirements of the ADA state that programs usually are not expected to make changes that are very difficult or expensive or that "fundamentally alter the nature of the services provided." If the alterations or changes needed to accommodate a child with a disability will be very costly and after an exhaustive search of community resources no less expensive alternatives are found, centers may be within their rights to deny admission to that child.

Larger centers with greater financial resources can afford to make more costly changes than smaller centers. A small center probably will not be expected to make substantial renovations to make its facility wheelchair accessible because those changes would not be "readily achievable." Hiring an additional staff person to care for a child with complex health care needs might be an undue burden for a small program with limited financial resources.

WHAT IF THERE IS A SEPARATE PROGRAM SPECIFICALLY FOR CHILDREN WITH DISABILITIES?

> Notwithstanding the existence of separate or different programs or activities provided in accordance with this subpart, a public accommodation shall not deny an individual with a disability an opportunity to participate in such programs or activities that are not separate or different. (PL 101-336, Section 302 [b][1][c])

Centers cannot deny services to a child with a disability even if a separate program specifically for children with disabilities is available. If a child with Down syndrome applies to your center, you may not deny him or her admission because there is a program next door that has services for children with Down syndrome, even if you feel that those services would be better for the child. Additional sections of the law prohibit denial of services or the provision of separate or unequal services except when necessary to provide a service that is as effective as that provided to others. In other words, the law repeatedly encourages inclusive settings.

In most cases it would be inappropriate for an early childhood facility to provide a separate service for children with disabilities. However, there would be some exceptions. For example, if the center sponsored several performances of a puppet show, a sign language interpreter could be hired for one performance and children and adults needing this service could be expected to attend that specific performance.

ARE CHILDREN EXPECTED TO PARTICIPATE IN ALL ACTIVITIES?

Under the ADA, early childhood programs must include children with disabilities in all activities. This means that creating a separate classroom for children with disabilities is prohibited. Centers must make provisions to ensure that children with disabilities can participate as much as possible in all program activities including field trips, special activities, and the playground.

◄o► ◄o► ◄o►

Juan, who has cerebral palsy, was doing well at Rainbow House. He was able to move around the classroom and seat himself at the table. The only time he had problems with balance was on the playground. The playground was sloped and covered with wood chips. Juan fell frequently and couldn't use the climbing equipment, the slide, or the riding toys. He could sit on the swing but would lose his balance when it moved.

The director met with Juan's parents and his teacher. They decided to contact Juan's physical therapist for ideas. The physical therapist visited the center and observed Juan on the playground. She suggested that the center buy a swing with a back support and a tricycle with higher handlebars, straps on the pedals, and a backrest. She also showed Juan's teacher how to help him go up the slide and sit down at the top.

The director purchased the new swing right away but she found out that the tricycle was very expensive. She just didn't have the money to buy it this year. Juan's parents were upset, but they talked with the physical therapist who suggested someone who could adapt a regular tricycle. This proved much less expensive than buying a new one and Juan worked hard learning to pedal.

In the fall when it was time to visit the Pumpkin Patch, Juan's teacher was concerned about how they would get around the fields so that he could choose his pumpkin and help pick apples. His mother suggested that they take a wagon that could be pulled through the fields. All of the other children took turns riding with Juan.

◄○► ◄○► ◄○►

Full participation for children with disabilities requires the resourcefulness and creativity of everyone involved.

IS THERE AVAILABLE FINANCIAL ASSISTANCE?

For programs that pay federal income taxes there are tax credits and tax deductions available to offset expenses associated with changes made to comply with the law.

A tax credit is available to small businesses for expenses incurred for the purpose of complying with the ADA. A tax deduction is available for "qualified architectural and transportation barrier removal expenses."

For more information on these tax provisions, order Publication 907 from your local Internal Revenue Service office. A local disability advocacy organization can tell you about other government assistance and/or tax benefits that might be available.

Nonprofit programs should check with local foundations, Kiwanis Clubs, Rotary Clubs, and other similar organizations to see if they can provide financial assistance to help defray expenses.

WHAT ABOUT INSURANCE?

Early childhood facilities may not deny admission to children with disabilities even if it results in an increase in insurance premiums or a cancellation of coverage. The ADA is very specific on this point because insurance requirements frequently have been used to exclude people with disabilities from a variety of programs and activities. This issue is difficult because the law does not require insurance companies to provide coverage. The issue of insurance is discussed in the regulations section (Sec. 36.212 3[c]).

If a program is faced with higher rates or a cancellation of a policy it eventually may have to sue the insurance company to compel it to prove that its actions are based on sound actuarial data. Insurance companies must base their rates on objective information. They must have evidence that a person with a disability is a greater insurance risk in order to raise their rates or cancel the policy. If your insurance company raises your rates, you should request that it provides you with information supporting its position that there is indeed a greater risk or likelihood of increased risk in serving children with disabilities. An insurance company does not have to tell the business it is insuring how the rates are established. If it appears that a particular insurance company has a common practice of discrimination, you could try contacting your state Commissioner of Insurance. If increasing numbers of programs are faced with this untenable situation, this provision of the law hopefully will be changed.

HOW IS THE LAW ENFORCED?

Under Title III of the ADA there are two avenues for enforcement. If a person feels that he or she has been discriminated against, a civil action for injunctive relief may be filed. Parents may file suits on behalf of their children who are minors. In cases of general public importance, the Department of Justice may intervene in the civil action. In some situations, the court may also appoint an attorney for the plaintiff.

If discrimination is found, the person may be granted a permanent or temporary injunction or a restraining order. In effect, an early childhood program can be ordered by the court to make alterations related to accessibility, provide an auxiliary aid or service, or modify a policy. Furthermore, when a complaint is filed, the court takes into consideration any good faith efforts to comply with the law. This means that an honest effort to accommodate children and adults with disabilities will count in favor of any early childhood program that finds itself in court. No compensatory or punitive monetary damages are awarded.

In cases where there is a pattern of discrimination or when the discrimination raises an issue of general public importance, the Department of Justice may bring a civil action. In addition to the penalties that apply in private suits, monetary penalties also may apply. For a first violation the court may assess a civil penalty not to exceed $50,000. Title III of the ADA (Public Accommodations) does not allow punitive damages.

The Department of Justice will investigate alleged violations of Title III. Individuals who believe they have been discriminated against or that a class of persons has been discriminated against may request an investigation. Where the Department of Justice has reason to believe that there may have been a violation of Title III, it may initiate a compliance review.

IMPLICATIONS FOR YOUR PROGRAM

Now that you have a general understanding of Title III of the Americans with Disabilities Act, you can begin to think about its implications for your program. Situations you may face as a provider include admitting a new child with a disability, making modifications for a child with a disability, and accommodating a parent who has a disability. Here are some sample circumstances you might encounter. As you read each of these examples, think about how you might respond. You also can use these scenarios in discussions with your staff. Listed before each situation are key concepts explained earlier in the chapter. You can refer to the glossary at the end of the book for the definitions.

When a New Family Enrolls

In the following conversation about enrollment, these issues related to the ADA are raised:

- Asking about a child's disability
- Addressing toilet training as an admission criterion
- Determining if the program includes children with disabilities

---

KEY CONCEPTS:
Nondiscriminatory admissions criteria

Mrs. Martinez calls to ask about enrolling her 3-year-old son Derek in a child care center near her job. She speaks with the director, Mrs. Sobel.

Parent:	Do you have any openings for a 3-year-old?
Director:	Yes, we have an opening in both our younger 3s and our older 3s. Would you like to come and visit?
Parent:	That would be great. By the way, do 3-year-olds have to be toilet trained?
Director:	Well, most of our 3s are trained. We work on it with some of the younger ones during the day.
Parent:	The reason I ask is because my son Derek is still in diapers. Would that be a problem?
Director:	I'm sure he'll get the hang of it soon, especially if you work on it at home and we work on it here.
Parent:	Actually he won't. He'll be in diapers for a while longer.
Director:	Oh, does he have a disability?

The director began by responding supportively, but she inquired directly about the child's disability. In accordance with the ADA, you may not inquire about the presence of a disability. She let the mother know that most of the children in the program were toilet trained by age 3, but she did not make it a condition of admission. Instead of asking directly about a disability, the director needs to consider whether this information is *necessary to the safe operation* of her program. Because, in this case it would not seem to be necessary, the director should not ask why Derek is not toilet trained.

Parent: Well, I wasn't sure if I should tell you but Derek has Down syndrome.

Director: We try to make our program a good place for all children. I'd be happy to talk with you about how we can work together to make this a good place for Derek. Can you tell me some more about him?

Parent: Derek's been in a special education program, but I think he's ready to be with regular kids. He just started walking a few months ago and he's trying to talk. I think it would be good for him to be around kids his own age so he can learn from them.

Director: It sounds like we have a lot to talk about. Please come visit, and if you decide that you want to send Derek here, we can sit down and decide how best to do that. It would be great if you could bring Derek for a visit so that we could get to know him. You know, our classes probably are larger than the classes he's been used to and our teachers haven't had any training on working with a child with Down syndrome. We'll count on you to tell us what we need to know.

The director learned about the mother's expectations of the program and responded supportively to her interests. She communicated important information about the center and set up a visit so that Derek's mother could decide if she wanted him to attend.

Parent: That sounds great! You're the first place I've called that hasn't sounded negative. Derek is really a sweet child and I know you'll like him. His special education teacher has offered to work with the program I pick to make sure the new people know what he needs.

This friendly exchange has laid the groundwork for a positive relationship. The director has given some basic program information—class size, ratios, and staff qualifications—and made it clear that the program did not have experience with children with Down syndrome or special education. She conveyed an accepting attitude and the mother made her appreciation clear. Many parents of children with disabilities meet rejection in this situation and may be afraid to disclose that their child has a disability. When they find a warm welcome they usually are eager to share information and resources to help the program work with their child.

When a Child Is in the Classroom

Sometimes, problems emerge after a child with a disability has been admitted. The next scenario looks at the continuing obligation that centers have to comply with all aspects of the ADA. It also focuses on

- Making all areas of the program physically accessible
- Making the kinds of accommodations that are possible
- Creating separate programs

KEY CONCEPTS:
Readily achievable, accessibility, undue burden, confidentiality

Angie, the teacher of the Monkeys (4-year-olds), demands to talk to Marsha, the director, about Sharon. Sharon has been at the center for just a week. She has cerebral palsy, wears braces on her legs, and uses a walker. She does not use the toilet consistently. On Friday morning Angie storms into Marsha's office.

Teacher: This situation with Sharon is not working out. There just are not enough adults to go around. Sharon requires so much time and I have to watch her constantly. Wednesday she fell twice and yesterday Jeremy pushed her and she cut her lip. She needs to be carried down the stairs and she can't do anything on the playground. I have to take her to the bathroom and then she has an accident and needs to be changed. It's not fair to the other kids. She can't do what they do. I really think another place that works with kids like her would be better.

Angie has pinpointed many problems. She is finding that the adult–child ratio is not working. She is worried about Sharon's safety and feels that the other children are being neglected. Angie thinks she does not have the skills or knowledge to teach Sharon, and she feels totally overwhelmed. Marsha needs to intervene quickly and supportively.

Director: Slow down, Angie. Let's take one thing at a time. You sound like you're at the end of your rope. Think for a minute, has anything with Sharon gotten easier?
Teacher: You know, Sharon is really a sweet little girl. I know she was scared on the first day. She is starting to talk to me more, and today for the first time she asked to go to the bathroom.
Director: This is a big adjustment for all of us, including Sharon. Let's talk and see what ideas we can come up with. If it means hiring an extra person, I'll just have to tell her mom we can't keep her. Our budget is too tight now.

Marsha has helped Angie step back and see some positive changes by offering a sympathetic ear and beginning the problem-solving process. Programs often think that hiring extra staff, which would create a financial hardship, is the only solution. Often, there are other, less expensive alternatives. The center needs to continue to exert every effort to find assistance and make reasonable modifications. If Marsha tries other ways to help Angie and Sharon and they don't work, she may decide that the only choice left is hiring an extra person. If she can show that this would be too expensive, she is within her rights to tell Sharon's mother that she can't afford it.

Angie had more worries.

Teacher: I'm still worried about the stairs.

Director: I've never considered this before but we could talk to Doris and see how she would feel about moving the Pandas (3-year-olds) up to the second floor. Then you could have her room and you wouldn't have to worry about the stairs.

Teacher: That would be great, but Doris might not like it.

Marsha and Angie have found a no-cost adaptation that would make life easier for everyone in Sharon's class. It will be simpler if Doris also sees the benefit. However, her objections really are not a legitimate reason to defer the move.

Director: Let me talk to Doris. I'm sure she'll agree when she understands the situation. I'm more worried about what's happening on the playground. We can't have Sharon getting hurt.

Teacher: Well, Sharon's walker doesn't work with the wood chips and she tips over easily. She really can't use any of the equipment by herself so she just stands and watches. Yesterday when Jeremy ran past and pushed her, she lost her balance, fell, and bit her lip.

Under the ADA, Sharon should be able to use the playground if she is to have full access to all the "goods and services" provided by the center. Safety is a primary concern. Both Sharon and the other children need to be able to play and learn in a safe environment. The center must look at ways they can safely make the playground more accessible. They also need to think about alternative outdoor accessible play areas they can use with the children.

Director: We've got to find a better way. Let's make a list of all our concerns. Then we'll see which ones we can solve ourselves and which ones we need to talk with Sharon's mother about. She told us that Sharon's physical therapist would help if we needed it. I think the public schools also have a resource center. In the meantime, I'll help supervise when you're outside and we'll try to come up with some things that Sharon can do.

There often are resources in the community that can help. Special education services in your local public school system may be available to answer questions. Your local chapter of The Easter Seal Society or chapter of United Cerebral Palsy Associations also may have information and materials. Seek them out and develop a list that is useful to you. The physical therapist may have ideas about how to make the playground safer and how to design activities in which Sharon can participate.

Teacher: There is one other problem. The other kids are starting to get used to her, but some of them tease her about her walker. How can I explain cerebral palsy to them?

Director: We could ask Sharon's mom to come in and talk to the class and she and Sharon could show how the braces and walker work. Also, I'll look for some books about disabilities that you can read to the class. You need to talk with the children and let them know that everyone is different and everyone belongs. They're old enough to understand that teasing hurts other people's feelings.

Children notice differences and it is important to give them accurate, concrete information. It is also important to respect each child's privacy. If Sharon's mother talks to the class, she is then giving the other children permission to talk about Sharon's disability and she is showing them how to do it respectfully.

Confidentiality is a critical issue. Centers may not disclose information about a child or a disability without prior permission. All information pertaining to a child's disability must be kept in a separate file and only persons with whom the parents have consented that the information be shared may have access to that information. Check your state's confidentiality regulations. Also, be sure to check with the parents and get their permission before you talk to the other children or families.

When a Parent Has a Disability

The ADA also applies to family members of children in your program who have a disability. You are responsible for ensuring that parents and family members, as well as other members of the community, have full access to your center. In addition to physical accessibility this also means adapting the way you communicate with families to meet the needs of someone with a visual or hearing impairment.

The following situation illustrates how one program made adaptations for a parent with a visual impairment.

KEY CONCEPTS:
Undue burden, auxiliary aids and services, accessibility

Director: Welcome to Kiddie Care. We're glad that your daughter will be joining us. Here's the application packet. Let's go through the papers together.

Parent: Could you read them to me? I can see a little, but I'm legally blind.

Director: Certainly. Let me just talk with the other parents and I'll be right back.

Reading the necessary materials is just as acceptable as having them available in braille. Accommodations don't have to be expensive. You do have to ensure that all program communications can be made accessible to people with disabilities. The best strategy is to ask the person directly how best to meet his or her needs.

Parent: Can you tell me about the papers you send home? I'm worried that I won't know what's going on at school.

Director: We send information home every week and the teachers post the schedule of activities outside their doors.

Parent: Would my daughter's teacher be able to call me with the information instead?

Director: Certainly, I'm sure we can work something out. Let's go talk with the teacher now so you can set up a schedule that works for both of you.

The director will need to follow up to make sure things are working out. She has done a good job of starting a positive relationship. Instead of worrying about how to make the modifications, she has taken the mother's suggestion. The teacher will need to be given adequate time to call the mother regularly, but once a schedule is established things should go smoothly.

2

Employees in Child Care Settings Under the ADA

KEY CONCEPTS:
Qualified individual with a disability, essential functions,
reasonable accommodations, undue hardship, direct threat

The purpose of Title I of the ADA is to ensure a person with a disability an equal position with all other people in regard to any employment practices or terms, conditions, and privileges of employment. This title is very broad and covers such areas as

- Applications
- Interviews
- Promotions
- Tests
- Termination
- Compensation
- Disciplinary action
- Leave
- Job training
- Benefits
- Layoff
- Recall

HOW DOES THE LAW AFFECT YOUR EMPLOYEES?

If a private early childhood program employs 15 or more people, it must hire and promote people with disabilities if they are qualified for the job. People with disabilities must be treated like any other employee. The employer's duty under the ADA is to consider the applicant or employee and make employment decisions without regard to that person's disability. However, the ADA in no way prevents employers from hiring the most qualified applicant for the job.

The ADA is not an affirmative action law and businesses do not have to hire a specific number of, or give preference to, people with disabilities. Only people with disabilities who meet the necessary requirements for the job are considered *qualified individuals with a disability* under Title I.

Determining Whether an Individual with a Disability Is Qualified

Title I of the ADA says that employers may not discriminate against a *qualified individual with a disability* who is an

> individual with a disability who, with or without reasonable accommodation, can perform the essential functions of the employment position that such individual holds or desires. (PL 101-336, Title I, Section 101)

To be protected by the ADA, a person must first meet the definition of an *individual with a disability*. This three-part definition is the same as the one used in Title III, Public Accommodations, and states that under the ADA an *individual with a disability* is a person who has *a physical or mental impairment that substantially limits one or more major life activities; a record of such impairment; or is regarded as having such an impairment.* (PL 101-336, Section 3)

After meeting the conditions of this definition, which is explained fully in the previous chapter, the person must then meet the qualifications for the job. An employer is not required to hire or retain a person who is not qualified for the position.

Step 1—Does the Applicant Meet the Prerequisites?   There are two basic steps employers should follow to determine if a person is qualified under the ADA. First, the employer must determine if the applicant meets the necessary prerequisites of the job, such as

- Education
- Work experience
- Training
- Skills
- Licenses
- Certificates
- Other job-related requirements (e.g., good judgment or the ability to work with other people)

For example, in deciding whether a teacher who has cerebral palsy is qualified for a head teacher position, an employer would determine if the person had an early childhood degree or the required educational background. If not, the individual would legitimately not be qualified. If a child care center requires that all head teachers have at least 2 years teaching experience, an applicant with a visual impairment who had taught for only 1 year would not be qualified for that position. This first step helps employers decide if a person with a disability is otherwise qualified.

Step 2—Can the Applicant Perform the Essential Functions of the Job? If a person meets the necessary job prerequisites, the second step in determining if a person is qualified under the ADA has two parts: 1) identifying the essential functions of the job, and 2) deciding whether the applicant with a disability can perform these functions, with or without reasonable accommodations. Making this determination is a key aspect of nondiscrimination under the ADA. It requires the employer to focus on job performance. In the past, many people with disabilities who could perform the essential parts of a job were denied employment because they could not do things that were only marginally related to the job responsibilities.

As with Title III, the definition of who is covered by this section of the law, Title I also includes those associated with people who have a disability. If an employer refuses to hire a parent of a child with a disability because of concern about absenteeism caused by illnesses related to the child's disability, this would be viewed as discrimination under the law. It protects him or her from discrimination based on the potentially false assumption that his or her relationship with the person with a disability will lead to poor job performance. However, this part of the definition does not require the employer to make accommodations in the job for people who have such a relationship, such as providing more sick and personal days. In this situation, the employee would be expected to fulfill all the regular requirements of the job.

Essential Functions

Essential functions are determined by the employer. They are tasks that are fundamental and necessary to perform in a given position. Applicants with a disability must have the skills, education, and experience required for the position, and be able to carry out the most important elements or essential functions of the job. If asked, the employer must make affordable and easily achievable changes or reasonable accommodations to enable an applicant with a disability to perform the duties of the job. To determine which functions are essential to a given job and which are marginal, the law directs employers to consider the following areas:

1. The duties in the written job description
2. The amount of time spent on specific tasks/duties
3. The duties performed by current and past workers in the position
4. The number of available employees among whom job functions could be distributed
5. The consequences if a job function is not performed
6. The terms of any collective bargaining agreement

An employer should define the essential functions in a written job description and be prepared to assess each applicant's ability to perform those functions. If an applicant can't perform an essential function, the employer must decide whether removing or changing that essential function would fundamentally alter the nature of the job.

For example, a job description for a teaching assistant may state that the person holding the job vacuums the classroom; however, the most critical function of the job is to assist the teacher with the children. If the vacuuming usually is done by the custodial staff, a person whose physical limitations prevent him or her from vacuuming but who is otherwise qualified to handle the basic function of assisting the teacher with the children would be considered qualified for the position.

Getting children out of the building in an emergency is vital to their safety and might be an essential job function for a classroom teacher. What if a person in a wheelchair applied for this job? Does the construction and layout of the building allow the individual to get the children out safely? Do some of the children need to be carried? Removing emergency evacuation from the job description probably does not change the nature of the job if it is a teaching position. If the employer decides that the applicant in the wheelchair is the best qualified for the position, he or she would have to consider what accommodations could be made to allow the applicant to participate in the program's evacuation plan. Some solutions might include developing an alternative evacuation plan for that classroom or assigning an additional staff person to assist during fire drills.

Reasonable Accommodations

Reasonable accommodations are any changes in the work environment or in the way the job usually is done that results in equal employment opportunity for an individual with a disability.

Employers must make reasonable accommodations to the known mental or physical limitations of qualified applicants or employees who have disabilities, unless they can show that the needed accommodation would cause an undue hardship on the operation of their business.

Reasonable accommodations include the following:

- making existing facilities used by employees readily accessible to and usable . . . ; and
- job restructuring, part-time or modified work schedules, reassignment to a vacant position, acquisition or modification of equipment or devices, appropriate adjustment or modifications of examinations, training materials or policies, the provision of qualified readers or interpreters, and other similar accommodations. (PL 101-336, Title I, Section 101 [9])

Employers are not required to make reasonable accommodations unless the need for an accommodation is obvious or the employee or job applicant makes a specific request. Many people with disabilities can perform jobs without any modifications or special assistance. But many others have been excluded from jobs that they are qualified to perform because of unnecessary barriers in the workplace. The ADA recognizes that such barriers may discriminate against qualified people with disabilities just as much as more obvious discriminatory practices. For this reason, the ADA requires employers to make reasonable accommodations as a means of overcoming the unnecessary barriers that prevent or restrict employment opportunities for people with disabilities.

Job Restructuring A situation you may encounter involves an employee who returns to the job following an illness or an injury. The resulting disability may be temporary or permanent and you will need to determine what job modifications should be made. Under some circumstances, a temporary disability, such as reduced mobility following hip replacement surgery, may be covered under Title I of the ADA. Each circumstance will need to be decided on a case-by-case basis.

Job restructuring may involve altering the hours worked or modifying the job responsibilities. If an employee needs a mid-day rest period because she takes medication that causes drowsiness, her work schedule could be modified (e.g., 7 A.M.–12 P.M. and 3 P.M.–6 P.M.). An employee who needs additional unpaid leave time for medical appointments may be able to work out a flex-time schedule. A teacher with a visual disability might require braille, large-print, or audiotaped materials.

For an employee with restricted mobility, nonessential job responsibilities could be reassigned allowing the employee to have duties as a receptionist instead of as a supervisor of the children on the playground. In one school, a teaching assistant with cerebral palsy had trouble walking long distances. Part of her job was to take the older children to a store nearby. Because she was well qualified and good with the children, her supervisor arranged for the teaching assistant from the next room to walk the children to the store. The employee with cerebral palsy went into the other classroom to help out for the duration of the walk. These modifications required thought and planning, but the school, the children, and the employee all benefited.

The best approach in these situations is to work with the employee to decide what, if any, reasonable accommodations need to be made. If you can make the accommodations easily, do so. If the accommodations are difficult or potentially costly, you will want further guidance on the requirements of the law before you proceed. Consult the Resources at the end of the book for further information.

Undue Hardship

Employers are not expected to make accommodations that would cause an *undue hardship*. This definition is similar to the readily achievable requirement for barrier removal in Title III. It is

> an action requiring significant difficulty or expense. (PL 101-336, Title I, Section 101 [10])

The law considers the following factors when making a determination of undue hardship:

- Size of the business
- Financial resources of the employer
- Cost of the accommodation
- Cost in relation to the size of the business and its resources
- How the accommodation would alter the business or the delivery of services
- Disruption to other workers

The determination of undue hardship must always be made on a case-by-case basis. The concept of undue hardship includes any action that is unduly costly, extensive, substantial, and disruptive or that would fundamentally alter the nature or operation of the business.

For some smaller child care centers, providing unpaid leave for an employee to attend medical appointments might constitute an undue hardship if substitutes for that employee are very difficult to find and expensive.

The best approach in dealing with these questions is to talk with the applicant or employee about practical and inexpensive accommodations. If it would be an undue hardship for you as an employer to pay the total cost of a needed accommodation, you may offer to pay the portion you can afford and you may ask the applicant or employee to pay the balance.

Direct Threat

Direct threat has the same meaning as in Title III,

> a significant risk to the health or safety of others that cannot be eliminated by reasonable accommodation. (PL 101-336, Title I, Section 101 [3])

Programs do not have to hire or employ individuals who pose a direct threat to themselves or to others. Employers must make the determination of direct threat on an individual basis. In determining that a direct threat is present, an employer must meet specific and stringent requirements. The employer must be prepared to show that there is

- Significant risk of substantial harm
- The specific risk must be identified
- It must be a current risk, not one that is speculative or remote
- The assessment of risk must be based on objective medical or other factual evidence regarding a particular individual
- Even if a genuine significant risk of substantial harm exists, the employer must consider whether the risk can be eliminated or reduced below the level of a "direct threat" by reasonable accommodation

The employer must attempt to alleviate the threat by making reasonable accommodations. Only then may he or she deny employment to an otherwise qualified individual with a disability.

For example, if an applicant with appropriate qualifications applied for a teaching position in the 2-year-old group and told her prospective employer that she had seizures, the employer might be concerned that she would have a seizure during work and injure either herself or a child in her care. The definition of *direct threat* in Title I includes a significant risk to the health and safety of the employee as well as to others. In this situation, the employer should carefully assess the likelihood of an injury occurring. If the applicant's seizures were well controlled, the possibility of injury would be slight. If, however, the applicant had several seizures a week, the risk of injury might be greater. Then the employer and the applicant must work together to see what accommodations could reduce the risk.

The outcome in this situation depends on several factors—how frequent and how severe the seizures are, and whether the applicant might fall or might drop a child she was carrying if a seizure occurred. Teaching other staff members what to do in the event of a seizure, preparing the children for that possibility, and determining that the chance of injury to the employee was slight could ensure the safety and well-being of all involved. If reasonable accommodations can significantly reduce or eliminate the possibility of injury, then the employer must consider hiring the applicant. If the employer feels that even with reasonable accommodations the applicant would endanger him- or herself or the children, the employer does not have to hire the applicant.

HOW WILL THE LAW AFFECT YOUR HIRING PRACTICES?

You will have to review your hiring process to make certain that it is not discriminatory. Be sure to review all written materials as well as any interview questions.

Job Descriptions

In addition to listing essential functions, job descriptions should carefully describe all the important aspects of the position. The first step is to identify the major responsibilities of the job. What are the key tasks the employee must perform? List each task and estimate the percentage of time spent on each responsibility. This list eventually will become the *essential functions*. Other tasks that are important but not essential may be listed under "nonessential functions."

Think about the physical demands of the job as you develop your list of essential functions. For example, being able to lift and carry children is an important part of a teacher's responsibility in an infant or toddler classroom. Specify how much time the employee is likely to spend performing each physical demand and the approximate weight the employee will be expected to lift. A job description for an infant teacher might include frequent lifting and carrying of children weighing approximately 14–30 pounds, but a job description for a substitute teacher who floats among several classrooms might include a weight range of up to 50 pounds to reflect the weight of children ages 2–5.

In addition to the physical demands of the job, it also is important to consider the mental demands, the general working conditions, the type of communication skills required, and any equipment that must be used. All important requirements should be included in the job description.

Writing a Job Description

The written job description should give the reader a clear idea of the scope of work required. It is not necessary to list all the specific tasks, but the major responsibilities should be defined clearly. Job descriptions should be updated regularly. It is a good idea to review the description before you advertise an open position.

A job description should include the following components:

Title
Use a short, descriptive name for the position.

Qualifications
This section states the minimum knowledge and skill level necessary to perform the job (e.g., education level, number of years of experience). Use the **ASK** principle to guide your writing: **A**bilities, **S**kills, **K**nowledge. The specifications should be consistent with your licensing standards.

Supervision
Provide the title of the supervisor to whom this individual reports.

Objective
This section describes the overall function and responsibilities of the job. It should be no more than one paragraph long and should complement, but not repeat, the job duties section.

Duties
This section states the specific job duties including the essential and nonessential job functions. List the duties in order of importance and include the percentage of time devoted to each major task. Try to keep the language clear and simple. It helps to begin each sentence with a verb. General nonessential tasks often are covered by including the phrase, "performs all other duties as assigned," at the end of the description.

See Figure 1 for a sample job description using these guidelines.

Application Form

The ADA prohibits employers from asking about the presence of a disability. The questions on the job application must be related directly to the applicant's ability to do the job. This means that

---

TITLE:
Teaching Assistant (Infant/Toddler classroom)

QUALIFICATIONS:
Must have a high school diploma or equivalent and an expressed interest in working with young children. Past experience in child care is preferred.

SUPERVISION:
Reports to the assigned Lead Teacher and adheres to all policies and procedures of the center.

OBJECTIVE:
Assists the Lead Teacher in planning and caring for all assigned children. Observes procedures and practices that promote and support the health and safety of all children at the center.

DUTIES:
A. Programming—75%
   1. Helps the Lead Teacher implement daily classroom activities and events
      a. **Interacts in a respectful and caring manner with the children by actively participating in their play and learning**
      b. **Frequently lifts and carries children weighing approximately 14–28 pounds**
      c. **Changes diapers and assists with toileting and hand washing**
      d. **Maintains a clean and safe environment for the children through general housekeeping practices such as washing tables, wiping spills, and cleaning toys and dishes**
      e. Prepares food for snacks and lunches
      f. Supervises children on the playground and during nap time
   2. **Assumes the primary teaching responsibilities in the absence of the teacher**
B. Planning and Preparation—20%
   1. **Meets weekly with the Lead Teacher to plan daily activities and schedule**
   2. Helps prepare materials for classroom activities
C. Administrative—5%
   1. Logs in attendance each morning
   2. Keeps records of children who received subsidized food from program
   3. Assists the Lead Teacher in keeping anecdotal records of children's daily activities and maintaining the files on each child
In addition to the duties stated above, the Teaching Assistant will perform all other duties as assigned by the Lead Teacher or the Center Director.

Figure 1.   Sample job description. Essential job functions are indicated in bold.

many questions that traditionally have been included in job applications are no longer allowed. The following is a list of unacceptable questions that may not be asked:

1. Have you ever had or been treated for any of the following conditions or diseases (followed by a checklist)?
2. Please list any conditions or diseases for which you have been treated in the past 3 years.
3. Have you ever been hospitalized? If so, for what condition?
4. Have you ever been treated by a psychiatrist or psychologist?
5. Is there any health-related reason you may not be able to perform the job for which you are applying?
6. How many days were you absent from work because of illness last year?
7. Have you had any major illness in the past 5 years?
8. Are you taking any prescription medications?
9. Have you ever been treated for drug addiction or alcoholism?
10. Do you have any disabilities or impairments that may affect your job performance?

All applicants should be given the written job description at the time of application.

Interviewing Job Applicants

All questions in the interview must pertain to the applicant's ability to perform the functions of the job. Employers are not allowed to ask about the health of applicants or about possible disabilities. Examples of acceptable questions include

Are you able to perform these tasks?
How would you perform the tasks?
What accommodation(s) do you feel you might need?

Instead of asking, "Do you have a mental or physical disability that would affect your ability to do the job?", you may ask, "Is there any reason that you cannot perform the essential functions of the job as listed below?" You also may ask, "Is there any reason that performing the functions of the job would create a danger to you or to others?" The rephrased questions avoid asking directly about the presence of a disability. Instead, they seek information about the applicant's ability to perform job-related functions.

Again, it is a good idea to give each applicant a copy of the job description before the interview. When you actually hire the applicant, you may review it once more, have the applicant sign and date it, and keep it in his or her personnel file. This way there can be no confusion about job duties and responsibilities.

Medical Exams

Medical examinations may not be required until after an offer of employment has been made and it must be a requirement for all employees. The offer of employment may be conditional; that is, applicants may be disqualified if they do not pass the exam. The medical criteria used in the exam must be job related.

For example, the medical form can include questions about the applicant's physical ability to move light furniture, get up and down from the ground easily, and lift and carry weights of up to 30 pounds if these are part of the essential functions of the job. The applicant can be disqualified only if he or she is unable to perform these functions even with reasonable accommodations.

In early childhood programs, the medical exam forms are often very brief and ask only if the applicant has active tuberculosis or other communicable diseases. If you must use a standard medical form, you may include a cover letter to the physician that details the essential functions of the job and asks if the applicant can accomplish these tasks with or without reasonable accommodations.

Confidentiality

Personal information on all employees always should be kept confidential. The ADA requires that any information about an employee's disability be kept in a separate and confidential medical file. Only supervisory personnel and emergency medical personnel may be informed about a person's disability, and then, only if it is medically necessary.

HOW IS THE LAW ENFORCED?

Title I is enforced by the Equal Employment Opportunity Commission (EEOC). A person who feels that he or she has been discriminated against may file a complaint with the EEOC; and after a "right-to-sue" letter has been issued, that person may bring a lawsuit directly against the employer. An individual, group, or organization also can file a charge on behalf of another person. A charge of discrimination must be filed with the EEOC within 180 days of the alleged discriminatory action. A charge can be filed in person, by telephone, or by mail. The procedures for processing charges of discrimination under the ADA are the same as those under Title VII of the Civil Rights Act of 1964, PL 102-166.

After a charge has been filed, the EEOC investigates. An investigation is started by reviewing information from the person making the charges and requesting information from the respondent. After receiving all the information from the investigation, the Commission sends an official "Letter of Determination" to the charging party and the respondent (employer), stating whether it has or has not found "reasonable cause" to believe that discrimination occurred.

If the investigation finds no cause to believe discrimination occurred, the EEOC will take no further action. The EEOC may issue a "right-to-sue" letter to the charging party who may then initiate a private suit.

If the investigation shows that there is reasonable cause to believe that discrimination occurred, the EEOC will try to resolve the issue through conciliation. At all stages of the enforcement process, the EEOC tries to resolve the issues without a costly lawsuit. Only when all other efforts fail does the EEOC file a lawsuit in district federal court.

If the court determines that discrimination has occurred, it may impose remedies that include the following:

- Reinstatement
- Promotion
- Back pay
- Front pay
- Reasonable accommodation
- Attorneys' fees
- Expert witness fees
- Court costs

Compensatory and punitive damages may be awarded when intentional discrimination is found. If an employer can demonstrate that a "good faith" effort was made to provide reasonable accommodations, compensatory or punitive damages are not allowed.

PRACTICAL APPLICATIONS

When a prospective employee contacts you, the first conversations are important. Typically, you want to find out about the applicant's qualifications, capabilities, and overall interest in the job. The following issues related to the ADA could arise:

- Inquiring directly about the presence of a disability
- Requiring a medical examination as a condition of employment
- Defining the *essential functions* of the job

The following dialogue between an applicant and a director illustrates some of the concepts related to employing a person with a disability.

KEY CONCEPTS:
Essential functions, reasonable accommodations

Applicant: Hi, my name is Peggy Lyle. I saw your ad in the paper and I'd like to apply for the Child Care Specialist position.

Director: That's fine. Do you have an Associate degree or a Child Development Associate credential?

Applicant: Yes, I have a C.D.A. and I'm working toward my B.A. in Early Childhood Education.

Director: Well, send me your résumé and we'll set up an interview. Could you also bring a health certificate that shows the results of a recent physical and certifies that you have no communicable diseases?

The director has been able to establish that the applicant has the necessary educational background for the job. This is very important because under the ADA you have the right to hire the most qualified person whether or not he or she has a disability.

However, when the director asked for the results of a medical exam she was going beyond what the ADA allows. You may require a medical exam only **after** you make a job offer and you must require the exam of **all** new employees, not just those who may have a disability. The offer of employment is final only after the applicant is found medically capable of performing the essential functions of the job with or without reasonable accommodations.

At the scheduled interview, the conversation continues.

Director: I'm pleased to meet you, Ms. Lyle. I'm Carol Williams, the director. Your résumé is very impressive. After you read this job description and our brochure, we'll talk.

Applicant: This sounds very much like the work I did in my last job.

Director: Well, you seem to have lots of experience. I'm a little worried though. I see you use a cane. Is there something the matter with you?

Remember that giving the applicant a written job description is always a good idea. This way there can be no misunderstanding about what the job entails. As mentioned previously, the job description should list the duties and responsibilities and identify those that are considered *essential*. You, as an employer, are allowed to ask how the applicant will be able to perform those essential job functions.

Although you may ask an applicant how he or she will perform the essential job functions, you may not ask directly about the presence of a disability. When the director saw that the applicant used a cane, she could have asked Ms. Lyle if she would need any accommodations to perform the duties of the job. As she does in the following conversation she also could have described some of the job tasks and asked if Ms. Lyle would be able to fulfill them.

Director: You know, this job is very physically demanding. The children need to be picked up and carried. I need someone who can keep up with them on the playground and take them on field trips. That class often walks to the park and the grocery store. Would you be able to do those things?

Applicant: Yes, I'm sure I could. I did many of the same things in my last job. If I use my cane for support, I can pick up a child with no problem. I walk a little slowly, but I don't have any trouble with short distances. I'll also visit the park and the store to be sure about any stairs or uneven ground.

Director: That sounds fine.

The director has described some of the *essential functions* of the job and has asked if the applicant would be able to do them. The applicant described how she could. If the director had further concerns, she could ask the applicant to demonstrate how she might pick up a child or supervise a group on the playground.

The applicant has not asked for any *reasonable accommodations*. She has indicated that she can fulfill all the job requirements. This means that no special modifications need to be made.

Applicant: I'd like to know about benefits. Do you offer paid sick and annual leave?

Director: Yes, we do. We also have health insurance, but I'll need to check and see if you can enroll. You may have to pay a higher rate because of your pre-existing condition. I'll also need to check with our insurance carrier about liability. I want to make sure we're covered if you have an accident.

Letting potential employees know about your benefits is important, and they have the right to ask. However, under the ADA, an employee with a disability is entitled to the same insurance coverage as all other employees. Concerns about insurance cost or coverage may not be used to deny employment. Instead the director should have gathered all the benefit and insurance information ahead of time so she could respond appropriately to the applicant's inquiries.

On-the-Job Training

Most child care centers offer some type of in-service training. As you plan and conduct your own training sessions, you should consider the communication needs of your staff. If you employ a person with a hearing impairment, you may need to secure the services of an interpreter to allow your employee equal benefit from the training session. A staff person with a visual impairment may require large-print or braille materials. Someone with a reading disability may need the training materials audiotaped.

Most of these accommodations are relatively simple and inexpensive, but they do require advance planning. Remember that your employees are entitled to equal benefits in **all** areas of employment.

3

Overview of Disability Laws

Section 504 and IDEA

KEY CONCEPTS:
Free, appropriate public education;
least restrictive environment; integrated settings

Until the 1970s, children with disabilities often had been denied access to public education. Both the civil rights movement and the efforts of parents of children with disabilities contributed to the passage of legislation that ensured their rights; and children with disabilities gained a mandate for education when federal legislation was enacted. PL 93-112, the Rehabilitation Act of 1973, Section 504, and PL 101-476, the Individuals with Disabilities Education Act (IDEA) of 1990, now guarantee a *free and appropriate, publicly supported education* in the *least restrictive environment* (LRE) to all children with disabilities. PL 101-336, the Americans with Disabilities Act (ADA) of 1990, is the most recent of the federal laws ensuring the civil rights of children with disabilities and prohibiting discrimination.

The related laws helped shape current thinking and programming for young children with disabilities. They have a major impact on the children with identified disabilities that you serve in your center. Knowing about these related laws can help you understand what you must offer and how you can locate the resources and services available for any child with a disability in your program. In 1990, an Urban Institute National Child Care Study estimated that approximately 6,500,000 children under age 5 in the United States were in full- or part-time care by someone other than a parent. Family child care homes and child care centers accounted for 64.5% (4.2 million) of the children. The Department of Education, Office of Special Education Programs (OSEP), reports that the incidence of disability in early childhood is estimated at 10%. Thus, about

42,000 children in child care could be in need of some type of special education services. There is the possibility that 1 of 10 children at your center may have a diagnosed disability.

According to incidence statistics from state special education departments, at least half of those children will have speech and language disabilities. The other half of those children will have a variety of disabilities, such as congenital anomalies, genetic disorders, neurological disorders, and sensory disorders. Many of these children are entitled to special education and related services. The following sections describe each of these related laws and compare some of their features.

PL 93-112, THE REHABILITATION ACT OF 1973, TITLE V, SECTION 504, NONDISCRIMINATION UNDER FEDERAL GRANTS

Title V of the Rehabilitation Act contains the following five sections:

- Two sections cover affirmative action for individuals with disabilities
- One section addresses accessibility in federal buildings
- One section addresses attorney's fees
- One section (Section 504) prohibits discrimination against individuals with disabilities by recipients of federal financial assistance

Impact on Education

Section 504 has the most substantial impact on education and child care. It defines a person with a disability, describes that person's civil rights, and outlines the legal recourse. In 1977, the regulations governing the implementation of Section 504 were signed. They provided that

> No otherwise qualified handicapped individual . . . shall, solely by reason of his [or her] handicap, be excluded from the participation in, be denied the benefits of, or be subjected to discrimination under any program or activity receiving federal financial assistance (PL 93-112, Title V, Section 504; CFR 104, Section 104.4[a])

This law defines a person with a disability as

> Any person who
>
> (i)   has a physical or mental impairment which substantially limits one or more of such person's major life activities,
> (ii)   has a record of such an impairment,
> (iii) is regarded as having such an impairment.

Major life activities include

- Caring for oneself
- Performing manual tasks
- Walking
- Seeing
- Hearing
- Speaking

- Breathing
- Learning
- Working

The law applies to people of all ages. The ADA definition of a qualified person with a disability is based on Section 504.

Policy of Nondiscrimination

This law is critical to the civil rights of people with disabilities because it prohibits discrimination. In any programs and activities that receive federal assistance, Section 504 ensures equal and accessible transportation, architecture, educational programs, and nonacademic services for children and adults with disabilities. Any child care programs receiving federal assistance, such as those on military bases or supported by the General Services Administration, may not discriminate against children, families, and employees with disabilities. All physical places (e.g., entrances, corridors, classrooms, play spaces, bathrooms) must be accessible and barrier free. Any transportation provided, such as buses or vans, also must be accessible for all users. Even if services to people with disabilities are separate, the quality of the services cannot be substantially different. Physical surroundings and transportation services must be comparable.

Enforcement

Agencies that have discriminatory practices face loss of federal funds, even if the funding is through indirect support. For example, an early childhood program that participates in a federal food program is receiving federal funds. Participation in the food program is in jeopardy if the program discriminates against children or employees with disabilities.

Child care facilities that comply with Section 504 already have many of the components in place to meet the requirements of the ADA. The Office of Civil Rights (OCR), U.S. Department of Education, is the enforcing agency for Section 504. There are 10 regional offices to answer questions, provide technical assistance, and investigate complaints (see Resources at the end of this book).

PL 101-476, THE INDIVIDUALS WITH
DISABILITIES EDUCATION ACT OF 1990

The groundwork for publicly funded educational programs for young children was laid out in the 1960s when programs such as Head Start were funded for children with and without disabilities living in poverty. Federal laws also provided funding to children with disabilities who were in state hospitals and institutions. Federal funding was authorized through grants for the development and demonstration of model services for children with disabilities. Educational services were not yet required, but the effectiveness of early intervention services was being documented through study and research, which strengthened the case for later federal initiatives for education.

In 1975, PL 94-142, the Education for All Handicapped Children Act of 1975, mandated federal assistance to states for the education of all children with disabilities. Amendments to this law in 1986, PL 99-457, the Education of the Handicapped Act Amendments, lowered the age of eligibility for special education and related services for all children with disabilities from age 5 to age 3 (Part B for 3- to 5-year-olds). It also established a discretionary program for infants and toddlers with disabilities and their families (Part H for birth to 2-year-olds). In 1990, PL 101-476 amended the law and changed its name to the Individuals with Disabilities Education Act. These laws and amendments are the federal policy that guides education and early intervention for infants, toddlers, children, and youth with disabilities. This law has eight parts, including Parts B and H of the act, which authorize funding for the education of young children with disabilities; Part B is a mandated program and Part H is an elective program. In all states, children with disabilities, ages birth to 21, are eligible for special education services under these programs.

HOW STATES PARTICIPATE IN IDEA

Each state is responsible for ensuring that education for children with disabilities meets the requirements of the law according to a state plan. Of the federal funding to the states, 75% must be passed on to local education agencies. Local districts must apply to the state with assurances that they will meet the requirements of the state plan. Funding may be withheld if requirements are not met.

For states to be eligible for federal funding under IDEA, they must have a plan that includes the following provisions:

- All children with disabilities, regardless of the severity of their disability, receive a **free appropriate public education (FAPE)**—at public expense.
- The education of children with disabilities is based on a **complete and individual evaluation and assessment** of specific, unique needs of each child.
- An **individualized education program (IEP)** or an **individualized family service plan (IFSP)** is drawn up for every child found eligible for special education or early intervention services, stating precisely what types of special education and related services, or the types of early intervention services, each child will receive.
- All children with disabilities are educated in the **regular education environment** to the maximum extent possible.
- Eligible children have the right to receive **related services** necessary to benefit from special education instruction. Examples of related services include physical, occupational, and speech-

language therapy; transportation; and support services such as audiology, counseling, medical diagnostics, service coordination, family training, and assistive technology.

- Parents have the **right to participate** in every decision related to the identification, evaluation, and placement of their children.
- There must be **parental consent** for any initial evaluation, assessment, or placement. Parents must be notified of any change in placement that may occur; must be included, along with teachers, in conferences and meetings held to draw up individualized programs; and must approve these plans before they go into effect.
- Parents have the right to challenge and appeal any decision related to identification, evaluation, and placement or any issue concerning the provision of FAPE to their child. These rights are spelled out clearly in **due process procedures**.
- Parents have the right to **confidentiality of information**. No one may see a child's records unless the parents give their written permission. The exception to this is school personnel with legitimate education interests.

HOW SECTION 504, IDEA, AND THE ADA ARE RELATED

Each law applies to different activities—Section 504 to federal activities, IDEA to education, and the ADA to both the public and private sector. They are enforced by a variety of departments including the Department of Education, the Equal Employment Opportunity Commission, the Department of Justice, and the Federal Communications Commission. All are intended to ensure equal rights and privileges to individuals with disabilities in the mainstream of society.

The Definition of Disability

Much of the ADA is based on Section 504. The ADA uses the same definition of an *individual with a disability* and much of the same language, but broadens the scope of the law beyond activities under federal jurisdiction to states, localities, and the general public. Both laws emphasize equal access for all people with disabilities. However, neither law specifies services that must be provided to individuals with disabilities. Table 1 shows a comparison of the laws of Section 504, the ADA, and IDEA.

The definition of a qualified individual with a disability in Section 504 and the ADA is quite broad. This definition differs from that found in IDEA. IDEA defines children with disabilities as those 1) who have been evaluated in accordance with the law's evaluation requirements; 2) who have been determined, through this evaluation, to have one or more specific conditions, such as mental retardation or hearing impairment; and 3) who, because of their disability, need *special education and related services* (i.e., specifically designed instruction to meet their educational needs). Because of the differences in definitions, a child may qualify as an individual

Table 1. Comparison of the laws

	Section 504	ADA	IDEA
Setting	Integrated settings	Integrated settings	Least restrictive environment
Definition of disability	General and comprehensive definition of qualified individual with a disability	General and comprehensive definition of qualified individual with a disability	Specific disabling conditions defined
Applies to	Federally funded grants and activities	Transportation State and local government services Public accommodations Telecommunications Employment	Public education
Enforcement	Office of Civil Rights, U.S. Department of Education	U.S. Equal Employment Opportunity Commission U.S. Department of Justice U.S. Department of Transportation Federal Communications Commission	U.S. Department of Education

with a disability under the ADA or Section 504 and not qualify for special education under IDEA. Nevertheless, schools still must provide accommodations that are independent from special education services.

Title II of the ADA says that state and local government agencies, including public schools, may not use discriminatory practices or prohibit access to goods and services for people with disabilities. For example, a child may need to use a wheelchair but not be in need of special education. That child is still entitled to full access to all the available goods and services under the ADA and Section 504, such as the use of an elevator or ramp in an educational program. The same would be true of a child who has special health concerns and attends regular classes. No special education services may be required, but changes in the class schedule or extra rest periods may be needed for that child. Remember, if a child is not eligible for special education services but qualifies as an individual with a disability under the ADA or Section 504, he or she is still entitled to *educational goods and services and accommodations* in an integrated setting appropriate to the needs of that child.

Inclusive Philosophies

The ADA and IDEA, despite different definitions of disability, are closely related. Both laws say that people with disabilities should be with their peers who do not have a disability as much as possible. The ADA states that

> Goods, services, facilities, privileges, advantages, and accommodations shall be afforded to an individual with a disability in the most *integrated setting* appropriate to the needs of the individual. (PL 101-336, Section 302, [B])

According to the ADA, no one with a disability should be made to choose a setting that completely separates him or her from others without disabilities. Segregated programs are not prohibited, but their existence may not prevent a person with a disability from participating in a more integrated setting. The creation of separate programs is actively discouraged.

If a parent wants his or her child who has a disability to attend a community program, the child cannot be denied enrollment because a separate program for children with disabilities is available. Within a building, the existence of separate special education classrooms for children with disabilities should not keep a child with disabilities from being included in a classroom with children without disabilities if that is the desired and appropriate placement. Both laws encourage programs in which people with and without disabilities are served together.

School systems often do not provide programs for typical children under kindergarten age. When such programs are offered, children with disabilities are entitled to be considered for inclusion in those classrooms. Because public school programs for typical children under the age of 5 are rare, families of young children with disabilities often turn to community early childhood programs, which now must abide by the ADA and provide integrated settings. But whenever the public schools offer programs for children at any age, they must provide those educational services in what is called the *least restrictive environment.* All states must establish procedures

> to assure that, to the maximum extent appropriate, children with disabilities, including children in public or private institutions or other care facilities, are educated with children who are not disabled, and that special classes, separate schooling, or other removal of children with disabilities from the regular educational environment occurs only when the nature or severity of the disability is such that education in regular classes with the use of supplementary aids and services cannot be achieved satisfactorily. (PL 102-119, Section 1412 [5][B])

If a public school proposes that a child spend most of the day in a separate special education class instead of a regular classroom, the school must prove that separate placement is appropriate. They must prove that modifications, auxiliary aids, and services were tried in the regular classroom and were unsuccessful. The positive and negative impacts on classmates, the teacher's time, and additional costs of the integrated placement also must be considered.

All three laws—the Americans with Disabilities Act, the Individuals with Disabilities Education Act, and Section 504 of the Rehabilitation Act—combine to prevent discrimination, ensure equal rights, and provide appropriate programs for all people with disabilities.

II

Making Inclusion Work in Your Program
Administrative Issues

Part II is designed to guide child care administrators in the process of complying with the ADA. Administrators are led through a detailed program review and compliance plan process. The issues of staff support and parent relationships also are addressed. Information is provided about special education services to assist administrators in child care settings in collaborating with their public school systems to obtain services and supports for children with disabilities.

4

Addressing Staff Concerns

Including children with disabilities in your program challenges the effort and commitment of everyone involved. As an administrator, your role is to develop a plan to bring your staff together, address their concerns, provide information and ongoing training, and identify community resources to support their efforts—it's quite a daunting undertaking.

Fortunately, you already do most of this on a daily basis; but because you are modifying your program practices, additional planning and preparation will be necessary.

Meetings with your staff serve two purposes. First, they provide a forum for people to express concerns. Second, they can lead to creative strategies you can put to use as you begin to evaluate your program and plan changes to ensure that all aspects of it are nondiscriminatory.

INTRODUCE THE IDEA OF INCLUSION

Bring the staff together to discuss the coming changes. Try to plan about five get-togethers so people have enough time for discussion as well as planning; if possible, schedule these get-togethers weekly. You can either extend the length of your regular staff meetings or you can schedule separate meetings. Allow about 90 minutes per session.

The main purpose of the first meeting is to give people an opportunity to express their concerns and feelings about including children with disabilities. Provide some background on the laws that require early childhood programs to be nondiscriminatory. Use the information and resources in Chapters 1 and 3 to get started. The National Association for the Education of Young Children (NAEYC) brochure, *Understanding the ADA* (1993), is an affordable introductory handout. Keep the information simple for now. You can buy other materials for your resource library that people can read later for more detail.

49

Typical Staff Concerns

Many staff concerns spring from negative societal attitudes and values about people with disabilities. Before your staff can welcome children with disabilities into your program, their feelings must be addressed and discussed. By bringing concerns out in the open, you let people know they are not alone in their doubts.

Larysa, the director of a large child care center, started her staff meeting by talking about the Americans with Disabilities Act as an extension of the civil rights protection afforded to many minorities.

◄o► ◄o► ◄o►

I remember as a child, feeling like I just didn't belong. After the first few days of kindergarten, I went home and asked my mother, "Where do the kids like me go to school?" My father was Indian and my mother was Latina. The children I went to school with were all White and this was the first time I realized I was different.

◄o► ◄o► ◄o►

Larysa's story led to a discussion among her staff of many childhood memories of not fitting in and being excluded. Encouraging people to share personal experiences promotes an empathic environment, and staff members begin to understand how the children in their care may feel.

You can start a discussion with your staff by asking them to remember a time in their childhood when they felt like they did not fit in.

"I remember being teased when I got glasses in third grade."

"I went to a birthday party in pants only to find all the other girls in party dresses."

Ask your staff members how they feel when they see a person with a disability.

"I was shopping and saw this man in a wheelchair trying to reach the soda. I didn't know what to do. Should I have offered to help, or would that have been too intrusive?"

"On a museum tour, a woman had braces on both legs and walked with crutches. It looked so hard for her to walk up a few steps. I caught myself staring and thinking how lucky I was."

"I was in a fast-food restaurant and the young woman wiping the tables had a disability. I didn't know people like her could hold a job. It was obvious that she took her responsibilities seriously."

As your staff begin to share these experiences they will find that they are not alone in their fears and they will begin to be more comfortable thinking and talking about children with disabilities.

"When we first started talking about people with disabilities, I was really uncomfortable. But as we talked more, I found out that I wasn't the only one who felt that way. Now that we've had these meetings, I feel closer to my co-workers."

By talking together, Larysa's staff were able to see that people with disabilities have been excluded regularly from many things that most people take for granted because of unfounded prejudices. They began to understand how much it hurt to be left out and labeled "different."

By the end of the meeting, Larysa's staff started to talk about wanting all children to feel welcomed, valued, and included.

WRITE AN INCLUSION PHILOSOPHY

Now that people have had time to think about inclusion, you can plan a meeting to talk about what inclusion will look like in your center. Does inclusion mean that any child with a disability could enroll? What about children with significant disabilities? What classroom should a child attend if he or she is chronologically 3 years old but not walking or talking? What about a child whose behavior is disruptive?

The Inclusion Survey in the chapter appendix is one tool you can use to facilitate this type of discussion. It includes hard questions like the ones above and asks each person to rate them according to personal belief.

Larysa used the Inclusion Survey at the beginning of the next staff meeting.

To begin your discussion, read each survey statement and ask people whether they agree or disagree. Because there are no right or wrong answers, people have the chance to hear their colleagues' reactions, clarify their own thinking, and begin to build a common core of beliefs that can form the basis of a mission statement for your program.

◄o► ◄o► ◄o►

I had each person fill it out privately. Then I put my staff in groups of three or four to talk about how they had filled out their surveys. Then we discussed the survey in a large group.

People had very different reactions to the survey. Some felt that any child should be included no matter what the disability. Others felt that sometimes it might be better for the child to be in a separate setting. Several people worried about how the other children would be affected. We decided to write a list of things we believed were central to our mission of providing good care for all children.

- *We believe that children with and without disabilities are more alike than different.*
- *We believe that all children have the right to the best possible care and education.*
- *We believe that all children are different and that those differences should be acknowledged and honored.*
- *We believe that children with and without disabilities can learn from each other.*

After we wrote the list, I had my staff work in small groups to write a few sentences about what inclusion should mean in our program. We came up with the following mission statement for our center:

"We believe that all children deserve the chance to grow and learn together. Our program provides a safe and nurturing setting that respects the individuality of each child and fosters self-esteem. All children are valued and appreciated for who they are. We help all the children in our care develop to their full potential."

We decided that from now on decisions about children and families in our center would be consistent with this new mission statement. We printed our new mission in the parent newsletter and made inclusion the topic of our next parent meeting.

IDENTIFY FEARS AND CONCERNS

The next step is to help your staff identify their concerns and develop strategies to address them. This can be done in a brainstorming session. Encourage each person to be honest. List the issues on a large piece of paper.

At the next staff meeting, Larysa asked her staff to describe their fears about inclusion. After some hesitation, many people participated. The list included the following concerns:

- Teacher–child ratios
- Sufficient time for each child
- Safety
- Special equipment
- Fear of hurting the child with a disability
- Lack of knowledge about disabilities
- Uncertainty about how to teach a child with a disability
- Potentially negative reactions of the other children and parents

Alicia was afraid that a child with a disability might get hurt and the parents would blame her. Ricardo felt that such children would be better off in a program with specialists trained to help them. Michelle thought that a few parents might leave the program because they wouldn't want their child around someone with a disability.

After everyone had a chance to talk, I asked them to work in small groups and come up with some creative solutions. After each group had talked together for about 15 minutes, I brought the whole group together and wrote all the ideas on another big sheet of paper.

◄o► ◄o► ◄o►

In-Service Strategies

The ideas generated by Larysa's staff included having a series of workshops to learn more about specific disabilities, special education services, teaching techniques, and program adaptations. People asked to visit programs that already included children with disabilities as well as programs that provided special education services. They wanted to learn more about the resources in the community. They also wanted to meet any children who might be planning to enroll and have time to talk with parents before their first day. These are all excellent strategies to use as you get ready for inclusion.

DEVELOP A PLAN

Larysa consolidated the groups' ideas for learning more about specific disabilities, special education services, teaching techniques, and program adaptations.

◄o► ◄o► ◄o►

I took all the ideas, summarized the issues, typed them, and gave a copy to each staff member. At our next meeting, I presented a preliminary plan for the coming year. Because there were several issues to be addressed, I asked for volunteers to form a committee for each issue. My staff were eager to get started and we had a lot of volunteers. We established a committee to coordinate four workshops during the year; a committee to review the admissions policies and establish new placement procedures, including time for the staff to visit other programs; and a committee to investigate community resources that could support their inclusion efforts. I promised that each committee would have 2 hours each week to meet together. No one really felt that 2 hours was enough time, but everyone agreed that with our busy schedules more time just wasn't realistic.

◄o► ◄o► ◄o►

The workshop committee should get everyone's input to decide which topics to address first. Learning about specific disabilities and finding out about community services are good first topics. Parents are important allies and supports as you move toward inclusion. Inviting a few parents who have children with disabilities to do a presentation is a good way to learn about the family perspective.

As you review your current admissions policies, check again to be sure they comply with the ADA. Chapter 5 includes a sample admissions policy that you can use as a guide. Build in time for staff and parents to plan a smooth transition into the program. This preparation lays the groundwork for successful inclusion experiences for children, staff, and families.

Follow-up is very important. Each committee should report back to you, establish reasonable time lines, and adhere to them. The workshop committee will meet all year planning and coordinating the training sessions. The policy review group can finish their work in about 3 months. Community resources should be updated on a regular basis, but a preliminary listing can be completed within a few months. Your preliminary list should include the special education resources in your public schools as well as the disability organizations in your community, such as The Arc (formerly the Association for Retarded Citizens), PODS (Parents of Down Syndrome), Easter Seals, the Association for Children with Learning Disabilities (ACLD), and United Cerebral Palsy Association, Inc. After each committee has met several times, it should review plans and progress and decide what needs to be done next. Keep the lines of communication among members open, and make sure everyone on a particular committee is aware of group activities and objectives. It is a good idea to review the entire plan at least once a year and modify it as your needs change.

EXAMINE YOUR PROGRAM STRUCTURE

Before you begin to include children with disabilities in your program, think about your overall program structure and your curriculum. Can your program accommodate the needs of children with widely varying abilities? How can you increase your ability to meet the needs of all the children and at the same time build in support for your staff?

◄o► ◄o► ◄o►

I had always felt that my center was based on practices that were developmentally appropriate. We even were accredited by NAEYC.

I had gone through the self-study process and received accreditation from the National Academy of Early Childhood Programs last year. But now I was facing new issues. How could I design my classrooms to meet a range of developmental needs? Could one class accommodate verbally precocious 3-year-olds, a child who was nonverbal, a child who was painfully shy, several very active and well-coordinated climbers, and a child who used a walker?

◄o► ◄o► ◄o►

Multi-age Groupings

One solution to accommodating children at different developmental levels is multi-age groupings. Instead of having groups of only 2-, 3-, and 4-year-olds, arrange classes with children ranging in age from 2 to 3, or 2 to 4. In each class there will be several children in each age range. Montessori classrooms have always had multi-age groupings, often with children from 3 to 5 years in one room.

Although your state licensing standards may be written for single-age groups, you can talk with your state or local licensing agency to see if it will permit multi-age groupings and adjust ratio and group-size requirements accordingly.

Team Teaching

Another creative approach to teaching diverse groups of children is team teaching. By pairing the 2-year-old class with the 3-year-old class for several activity times throughout the day, you can increase the options for children grouped both chronologically as well as developmentally. The two teachers can offer a variety of activities and the children can choose according to their interest. This way total group size is not increased and the teaching staff can coordinate their efforts.

Larysa decided to try the team-teaching approach. Three of her teachers already worked very closely together.

◄○► ◄○► ◄○►

Janice, Leticia, and Diane met and decided to try several combinations during the day. Janice and Leticia would have playground time together allowing the 2- and 3-year-olds to have a joint play time. Diane and Leticia would combine the 3- and 4-year-olds for story time and music. Diane and Janice decided to start a "buddy" program using volunteers from the 4-year-olds to "help" the 2-year-olds during art activities.

Janice commented, "At first the changes were time consuming for us and confusing for the children. But by the middle of the second week, things were running smoothly. I especially like our "buddy" program. It's really neat to watch the 4-year-olds helping the 2-year-olds glue and color. They're more patient than I would have imagined and the 2-year-olds really love the attention."

◄○► ◄○► ◄○►

These combinations allow the children to experience a wide developmental range of activities. Children are free to work on activities that match their developmental needs and interests. They also give the mature 4-year-olds the opportunity to be helpers. Children often do not have a chance to really help, and being a "buddy" can boost the self-esteem and skills of both the "helper" and the "helpee."

In addition, this team-teaching approach provides support for Janice, Diane, and Leticia. It gives them a chance to share ideas and discuss problems. It also reminds them that they are not alone.

CREATE TEAMS

No matter what you decide about your program structure, you need to establish classroom teaching teams to accomplish your program goals. Including children with disabilities is a challenge and teachers benefit from the support and shared responsibilities. By creating strong classroom teams, establishing specific roles and responsibilities for each team member, and scheduling regular meetings to discuss how the team is working, you can create an important support system for your staff.

◄०► ◄०► ◄०►

When I saw how well Diane, Janice, and Leticia were doing, I decided to create teams in all the classrooms. At first, people were confused about who should be on a team and how decisions would be made.

◄०► ◄०► ◄०►

The classroom team should be responsible for deciding how the classroom runs. If you decide to pair two classrooms full time or part time, the staff from both classrooms would form one team. The team should include the teachers, the teaching assistants, any volunteers, the program director or assistant director, and any specialists or consultants who are working with a child in the room. Other individuals should be invited to participate in team discussions as needed. For example, when the team is planning to discuss changing a child's classroom, the parents should be included in the meeting. Your support staff are valuable team members too, so remember to include the administrative assistant, bus driver, cook, or custodian as needed. Four to six people on a team generally works well. Keep the team small so everyone can contribute. The team still can meet even if one person is absent.

Teams, by definition, need to work closely together. When you begin to think about teams, you may want to ask your staff to identify people they would like to work with. Allowing staff to select their teams will contribute to the likelihood of successful team relationships.

Getting Teams Started

Teams should schedule regular times to discuss each child in the room. They should talk about scheduling, placement, classroom activities, and anything else that affects how their room runs.

◄०► ◄०► ◄०►

The staff formed some teams that were multi-classroom and some teams that were single classroom. Diane, Janice, and Leticia had a big head start. They were used to talking with each other and they shared similar ideas about how to teach. But as they began to include their classroom assistants, several issues arose. Some of the assistants were hesitant to speak up. Ruth, who worked with Diane, suggested that everyone on the team have an equal voice. She felt that each person had a different point of view and that all opinions were valuable. The team agreed and the members began to relax.

◄०► ◄०► ◄०►

Effective teams do not develop overnight. They need clear goals and rules for functioning. Meet with each team and help the participants think through the guidelines that will work for them.

Each team has to decide how it will make decisions. Some people decide to vote; other people discuss an issue until all participants agree. Basic ground rules help each team's productivity and reduce frustration.

Team meetings should last about an hour. An agenda, developed in advance, can help ensure that all important issues are discussed. A notebook in the classroom is a convenient place for people to jot down concerns as they arise during the day. These ideas or concerns can become meeting agenda items. Other ideas can be added to the agenda at the beginning of the meeting.

Each meeting should start with a review of things that were discussed at the last meeting. Anyone with a pressing problem should be encouraged to talk about it first; then, the team can go on with the planned agenda. The meeting should end with a summary of what was decided. The summary reminds the team members of who said they would do what by when.

Someone should take notes at each meeting. These notes should then be copied and distributed. They are a good reminder of past discussions and they can be a quick way for people to catch up if they miss a meeting.

Supervisory Tips

People come to you when they have a problem and count on you to help. Your supervision and mentorship can provide important support when a staff person is in trouble.

◄o► ◄o► ◄o►

Denise, a teacher for the 2-year-olds, was worried about a child in her class. In the past week, Leyna, who had a visual impairment and wore glasses, had started pinching and pushing Jenna. Leyna and Jenna had always gotten along well. Denise had spoken with Leyna's mother and tried to keep Leyna and Jenna apart but nothing was working. She decided to talk with her director, Larysa.

◄o► ◄o► ◄o►

As a supervisor you can guide your staff through a problem-solving process. Right now, Denise needs more information. She needs to find out if there have been any changes in Leyna's life either at home or at school. Larysa can help Denise formulate the questions to ask. Is anything different? Is the pinching happening at a specific time or during a certain activity? Is it happening at home, too?

In addition to problem solving, you also provide important emotional support. Denise is worried and frazzled. She needs to know her concerns have been heard and that Larysa will work with her to solve the problem. Knowing that Larysa will always be on her side makes it easier for Denise to go to her.

◄o► ◄o► ◄o►

After talking with Larysa, Denise felt a lot better. She had figured out that Leyna was doing most of her pinching first thing in the morning and late in the afternoon. She spoke with Leyna's mother again and found out that Leyna's grandmother was very ill and Leyna's father was away visiting her. There had been quite a lot of upset in the family over the past few weeks. Leyna had started pinching her mother and crying when it was time to go to school.

Larysa and Denise talked again. Denise now knew that Leyna was upset and worried. She decided to help ease the transition in the morning by spending some time reading quietly with Leyna and Jenna before sending them off to play. In the afternoon she would remind Leyna that Mom would be there soon and give her some extra hugs. Larysa agreed with this plan and praised Denise for her sensitivity.

For the next week, Larysa checked in with Denise every afternoon. She provided encouragement as Leyna slowly began to improve. On 2 afternoons she stayed in the classroom to give Denise an extra 10-minute break. By the end of the week Leyna rarely pinched.

◄o► ◄o► ◄o►

Listening and problem solving are very important supervisory tools, but they are not enough. Your staff need to know that you will act promptly to support them and follow up regularly.

Any changes in your program should be communicated to your families. As you begin to include children with disabilities, it is a good idea to have a parent meeting to discuss the changes and answer questions. Ideas for conducting a parent meeting are included in Chapter 10.

Changes take time. Preparing to include children with disabilities and providing support to your staff are long-term endeavors. The staff meetings, workshops, and team meetings require creative scheduling to allot some hours during the workday and some after-work hours for these activities. Look to parents and other volunteers for assistance. Some parents may be willing to help in the classroom so a team can meet. Using volunteers during nap time can give staff time off during a day when they need to stay late for a workshop.

Even with extra help, these tasks can seem overwhelming. Remember, you do not have to do it all at once. You know your program best. Decide what is most important and start small.

Finally, as an administrator, you need support. Use the formal and informal networks available to you. Talk with other administrators about issues and ideas. Larysa meets with other program administrators on a regular basis.

◄o► ◄o► ◄o►

I really depend on my administrator network. We meet monthly to talk about licensing and business issues and we also give each other a lot of support. My friend Carla already has included a child with a visual impairment and a child with spina bifida in her center. Her staff were quite resistant at first, but now things are working well. Her positive experiences have given me the confidence to try inclusion in my own program.

◄o► ◄o► ◄o►

Many early childhood programs are facing the same dilemmas. You need regular reminders that you are not alone and that your efforts are for a good cause—quality care and education for *all* children.

Appendix

Feelings About Inclusion

The survey on the following page contains questions you can use in your group meetings to facilitate conversations about inclusion and child care.

Instructions: Read each statement. Then mark the column that indicates your agreement/disagreement. There are no right or wrong answers.

Statements	Strongly agree	Mildly agree	Mildly disagree	Strongly disagree
1. Some children with disabilities should not be in inclusive settings, even with extra help.				
2. The parents of a child with a disability should be able to decide what placement and services their child receives.				
3. Not all teachers of young children have the skills to work with children with disabilities.				
4. Children with disabilities should receive at least part of their education in a setting with typically developing children.				
5. For most children with disabilities, inclusion works only if there is extra adult help.				
6. A child with severe behavior problems can benefit from being in an inclusive setting.				
7. I would like to have children with disabilities in my setting.				
8. Inclusion is good for children with disabilities, but the other children usually do not benefit.				
9. Teaching children with disabilities is much harder than teaching typically developing children.				
10. Some children who are in inclusive settings would be better off in separate, more specialized settings.				

5

Program Changes

KEY CONCEPTS:
Self-study, compliance plan

Now that you have a working knowledge of the Americans with Disabilities Act, you may feel overwhelmed by the prospect of making the changes in your programs to comply with the law. Where should you start? How much should you try to do? If sufficient resources and time are available, the most thorough and efficient approach is to form an ADA work group to conduct a self-study. This is a review of all aspects of your program, including physical accessibility, programming and services accessibility, staff development, and available outside resources. The information collected in the self-study can be used to develop a *compliance plan* that will guide future changes. A comprehensive program review like this may feel like it is beyond the manpower and time that your program can afford. Even though this entire process may not be feasible for some centers, any administrator can use this systematic approach to think about what *can* be done. Planning changes to comply with the law is essentially a think, plan, do, and review process. The extensive process is outlined in this chapter. Choose the parts that are within your program's capabilities and make a start.

The appendix to this chapter provides some examples of potential accessibility problems relevant to the classroom and playground, and may constitute a plan for change.

HOW TO IMPLEMENT CHANGES IN YOUR PROGRAM

As you begin to think about what changes you may need to make to your program, it is often hard to decide where to start. The following suggestions can help you organize your efforts.

Create an ADA Work Group

The purpose of this ADA work group is to review the entire program for compliance with the law, to identify changes that are needed, to examine how changes can be made, and to monitor progress toward completing the changes. This group can be convened by anyone in a leadership role in your program, such as an administrator or a member of a governing board.

The group members should include, at minimum, a teacher, parent, administrator, and one person who has a disability or who represents an advocacy organization for people with disabilities. The person with a disability or the advocacy representative will be able to examine your program to help you identify changes that might otherwise be overlooked. The group needs to define the self-study task. How extensive will it be? What is a reasonable amount of time and effort to spend and still do a thorough job?

◄◦► ◄◦► ◄◦►

As the director of the Children's House, Ms. Adams wanted to make sure she was in compliance with the Americans with Disabilities Act. She already had attended a workshop about the particulars of the law and talked to her staff about including children with disabilities in the program. Most felt they could handle some children with special needs; there were children at the center who already needed special attention. They also wanted to know what the law required. Would they need to alter the buildings and classrooms? What if the changes were very expensive? Would the children with disabilities take too much time away from the other children because of their needs? Did they have enough teaching experience and knowledge to work with children with disabilities? Would they do more harm than good for the children with disabilities?

Ms. Adams decided to ask staff and friends if they knew anyone who could offer advice on how to proceed. She called the local chapter of The Arc, and one of its community outreach workers said she would help. Ms. Adams then convened an Americans with Disabilities Act work group consisting of two teachers, a parent, and the community outreach worker from The Arc.

At the first meeting, the group decided to review the center's philosophy and revise it to include a statement welcoming all children with and without disabilities. The group also decided it needed to find a way to examine the program to see that it met the requirements of the law. The group began to make a list of things to review.

◄◦► ◄◦► ◄◦►

Establish a Time Line

The ADA work group needs to develop a realistic schedule for completing a self-study and developing a compliance plan to implement the proposed changes. It also should set a deadline for completion of its work. Because the law is already in effect, the review of the physical accessibility and possible program adaptations should be completed as soon as possible (no more than 3–6 months).

Develop a Policy Statement

This statement reflects your program's commitment to the spirit of the ADA. Any new written policy should be reviewed by the appropriate governing board of your program. Most programs already have a philosophy, mission statement, or program description that will need only simple revisions. The following example of a program philosophy includes a statement of nondiscrimination with reference to including individuals with disabilities.

The Children's House is a child development center that seeks to provide a caring and supportive learning environment for children, ages 3 months to 6 years. The curriculum used promotes the social values of sharing, cooperation, and friendship. All children are helped to develop positive self concepts and to develop tolerance and understanding for others from different backgrounds. The school admits students of any race, color, differing abilities, national and ethnic origin, gender, or creed. The rights, privileges, programs, and activities are made available to all students and their families. The school does not discriminate on the basis of race, color, national and ethnic origin, gender, creed, or disability in the administration of any policies or programs.

THE SELF-STUDY

Thinking about the areas you might need to change is a good start. Now that you have reviewed your program beliefs and established an ADA work group, you are ready to move on to the planning and evaluation stage of the self-study.

Identify the Topics for Your Self-Study

The ADA work group needs to start by identifying aspects of the program that need to be reviewed. To comply with the ADA, a center should be as physically accessible as possible, and all the goods and services provided should be available to participants and employees with disabilities. To comply with the spirit of the law, it is important that all staff understand the law and develop some awareness about disabilities. It also is important for a center to identify resources in the community that can help provide information and technical assistance about people with disabilities and the ADA. These four areas should be the minimum objectives included in the self-study. The ADA work group should review each of these program aspects thoroughly. Other topics specific to your program should be added at your discretion. Figure 1, adapted from the ADA requirements, is an example of a self-study outline.

Conducting a self-study will help you decide what changes your program needs to make. The following steps describe the self-study process and lead you through the development of a compliance plan.

Gather Information

An important first step is to obtain documents that already exist and can help you in the self-study process.

Collect Floor Plans and Exterior Drawings   Floor plans and sketches of the exterior of the buildings are very helpful for the physical accessibility study. If you do not have the plans, use graph paper to sketch the layout of all interior and exterior spaces used by your program. Make notes on the sketches or plans as you do the study.

A. Physical accessibility

　　1. Entrances, hallways, stairways
　　2. Other access to goods and services (e.g., classrooms, play spaces, cafeteria, meeting rooms, playground, staff lounge, offices)
　　3. Access to restrooms
　　4. Other necessary measures

B. Program adaptations

　　1. Classroom
　　　　a. Schedule
　　　　b. Curriculum
　　　　c. Room arrangement
　　　　d. Equipment/materials
　　　　e. Placement/promotion
　　2. Transportation
　　　　a. Vehicles
　　　　b. Parking
　　　　c. Sidewalks
　　3. Communication—auxiliary aids and services
　　4. Written materials
　　　　a. Policies and procedures
　　　　b. Brochure/program information
　　　　c. Parent information
　　　　d. Operating procedures
　　　　e. Forms
　　　　f. Other written materials

C. Staff awareness and training

　　1. Knowledge
　　2. Needs
　　3. Training plan

D. Resources

　　1. Disability resources
　　2. ADA resources

Figure 1.   Outline of self-study for assessing physical accessibility and program adaptations.

Obtain a copy of the Americans with Disabilities Act Accessibility Guidelines (ADAAG) available from the Architectural and Transportation Compliance Board (see Resources at the back of this book). These guidelines are the standards for all construction of new facilities and will help you evaluate your existing building. Standards specific to facilities for children are currently under development. In the interim, the ADAAG should be your guide.

Collect All the Written Program Materials Include all the written program materials for your self-study, such as your policies and procedures, brochures, program information, parent handbook, operating procedures, any enrollment forms, application forms, medical forms, and job descriptions.

Completing the Self-Study

You now have gathered all the information and materials you will need to proceed with the self-study. The following section will lead you through the process.

Assess the Physical Accessibility Assessing the physical accessibility of your program will take time. You may wish to hire a consultant, such as an architect or someone with experience in universal design. The Architectural and Transportation Compliance Board and the regional Technical Assistance Center of the National Institute on Disability and Rehabilitation Research are good resources. The ADAAG contains all the required measurements for physical accessibility.

You will need copies of an accessibility checklist (a copy can be obtained from the U.S. Department of Justice [see Resources at the back of this book]), a clipboard, pencils, and a flexible steel tape measure. First, look at each space from the perspective of someone with mobility difficulties who may need special support to walk or may be using a wheelchair. For example, there should be adequate space for a person using a wheelchair to move around. Are walkways, doorways, and paths wide enough? Are sinks or table surfaces low enough to be within reach?

Next, assess each space from the perspective of a person with a sensory impairment. If a person is deaf or has a hearing impairment, are there enough signs or visual indicators? If a person has a visual impairment, are there tactile or auditory cues that the person can use to find his or her way around the building. Could you add increased visual contrasts or larger signs to help the person be more aware of the environment? Actually walk or move through each space to assess it. Use the accessibility checklist to make sure that you have completed a thorough study of the physical environment. Note areas that need improvement and record your findings. Figure 2 is a sample of a self-study checklist addressing physical accessibility.

Making Program Adaptations The following are guidelines for assessing changes in the classroom, transportation, communication, policies and procedures, staff, and resources.

Area	Time line/ Review date	Person responsible	Changes needed
A. Physical accessibility			

1. Entrances, hallways, stairways
  2. Other access to goods and
     services (e.g., classrooms,
     play spaces, cafeteria, meeting
     rooms, playground, staff
     lounge, offices)
  3. Access to restrooms
  4. Other necessary measures
	Begin ASAP;
	complete in
	6 weeks;
	review
	annually
		Consultant;
		program
		director
			1. Meets code
			2. Meets code
			3. Meets code;
			   furniture needs
			   rearrangement
			4. Need accessi-
			   bility signs

Figure 2.   Sample of self-study checklist addressing physical accessibility.

Changes in the Classroom   The specific changes you make in your classroom will depend on the needs of the children and families with disabilities in your program. Interview classroom staff members who have had previous experience working with children with disabilities and see what suggestions they have. Try to visit programs that include children with disabilities, such as a preschool special education program and an inclusive community program. Talk to the staff in those programs and get their suggestions; then, develop some preliminary ideas about ways to accommodate children, staff, and parents with a variety of disabilities in each classroom. Think about the materials and equipment in your classrooms.

- Do they offer a variety of opportunities to use all the senses—auditory, visual, and tactile?
- Does the curriculum allow for individualized teaching with flexibility to meet a variety of learning needs?
- Is there a schedule that is predictable for the children and reflects little "down" or waiting time?
- Are the blocks of time in the classroom schedule developmentally appropriate for the group?
- Is the classroom schedule flexible enough to accommodate programming changes?
- Are the major pieces of furniture in the classroom fixed so that a child with a visual impairment can develop an "internal map" of the room?
- How and when do children move from one activity to the next? Do they use bells, verbal directions, or lights? Do these strategies reach all the children?
- How will you provide access to special program activities (e.g., field trips)?

Figure 3 is a sample of a self-study checklist that looks at these concerns.

When a child enrolls in your center, another issue that must be addressed is placement. The same procedure that is used for all

Area	Time line/ Review date	Person responsible	Changes needed
B. Program adaptations			

1. Classroom
    a. Schedule
    b. Curriculum
    c. Room arrangement
    d. Equipment/materials
    e. Placement/promotion
	Begin ASAP; finish in 8 weeks; review with each program evaluation	Teacher and assistant; director will call and schedule visit to early intervention program	a. OK, schedules can be adjusted by teachers
			b. OK, curriculum has multilevel adaptations
			c. OK, room arrangement can be changed to suit needs of students; some rooms are very small
			d. Need toys with more tactile and auditory appeal; get books showing disabilities; do we know anyone who can adapt toys? Early intervention program says we can call them with questions!
			e. All children *must* move each year to next group. Is this a good policy?

Figure 3.   Sample of self-study checklist addressing classroom changes.

children should be used if a child has a disability, but there are also additional considerations.

To remain fiscally sound, most centers must operate at capacity and fill vacancies as soon as possible. In some centers the program director makes the placement decision. Other centers use a team decision-making process. Parents may request teachers, but they usually do not have a real part in the decision-making process.

Spaces usually are determined by chronological age. For example, infants and toddlers, 2-year-olds, 3-year-olds, 4-year-olds, and 5-year-olds are the traditional groupings. Some centers do have multi-age groupings, but still maintain a specific census by age in order to maintain good staff–child ratios. Children move on an annual basis into the next age group.

Although children with disabilities may not be at the same developmental level, it is generally recommended that they enter and stay with a group that is chronologically close to their age. For inclusion to be successful, it is very important that a child be integrated with his or her peers. When children enter group programs, they make friendships, and not moving with their group means losing those friendships. Even though a child may not progress on par with his or her classmates, it is important for the staff to recognize that a child needs to move on and have other teachers and learning experiences.

Chronological placement is not always an easy decision, and there can be difficult issues to confront. Sometimes a child is not toilet trained. Diaper-changing facilities and a free staff person may not be available with an older age group that typically does not have children in diapers. However, placement decisions should not be based on whether a child with disabilities is toilet trained. Generally, centers will need to make the necessary modifications to include that child appropriately. Call your licensing division if your state has regulations that prohibit children who are not toilet trained from attending programs. Out-of-date regulations must be changed to reflect the requirements of the ADA.

When a child with a disability lags behind his chronological peers, there is the inclination to keep him with other children at the same developmental level. This can present problems. For example, a 4-year-old who stays in a toddler classroom because of delayed development may pose a danger to the younger children because he is larger and stronger than the other children. Placing this child with other 4-year-olds helps him learn appropriate behaviors. The child hears more advanced language and can model more advanced social skills. The other 4-year-olds can act as buddies, helpers, and role models.

In some cases, children with disabilities will progress very slowly developmentally. If placement is decided solely on the basis of developmental progress, a child could remain in the same classroom for several years. Even though a child's development is slow, it is not appropriate for him or her to remain in a toddler classroom for 3 years.

In some school systems a child may attend a special education program and receive care before and after school in a regular setting. When a child attends two programs or has a dual placement, there are additional issues. In this situation it is consistent, open communication among both programs and the family that is critical. Any dual placement means that a young child with a disability must cope with the transition between programs, a larger number of staff with whom to interact, different curricula, and different rules. A child may be with other children with disabilities in the morning and then with typical peers in the afternoon.

There are many variables that need to be considered as you decide on appropriate placement. It may be helpful to begin with an expectation of chronological placement and work from there. Information about the child, the characteristics of the center, and the desires of the parents all need to be taken into account. Placement decisions should be made on an individual basis with input from all concerned.

Changes in Transportation This section should focus on making whatever transportation the program provides accessible to children and adults with disabilities. Entrances, sidewalks, and parking lots also need to be evaluated for accessibility.

- Are entrances wide enough? Are sidewalks clear of obstacles, without unusual drop-offs, and not too steep?
- Is there a clearly designated parking area close to entrances for an individual with mobility difficulties that is wide enough to accommodate a lift?
- Can vehicle seats accommodate a child with poor sitting balance? Are special seats available?
- Can a wheelchair or special chair be transported?

Figure 4 is a sample of a self-study checklist that looks at these concerns. Again, refer to the ADAAG standards to guide your study.

Changes in Communication People with hearing, visual, learning, or speech impairments may need adaptations and accommodations to enable them to communicate effectively. For example, someone with a hearing impairment who lip reads always must be seated close enough to see the speaker. Ensuring effective communication also may require the use of auxiliary aids and services. These aids and services can include sign language interpreters, note takers, large typewritten materials, and assistive listening devices.

Think about some possible alternatives to written and spoken communication that children, families, and employees might use.

- Can desk and pay telephones be reached easily?
- Are the telephone buttons or dial legible for those with a visual impairment, or is the enlargement of touch-tone buttons needed?
- Is sound amplification needed?
- Does your program distribute a large amount of printed material that may require the use of a reader or a reading machine for an individual with a visual impairment?

Figure 5 is a sample of a self-study checklist that looks at these concerns.

Changes in Written Materials Written policies and procedures are essential to the operation of any good organization. They guide the accomplishment of the mission and goals of the organization.

Area	Time line/ Review date	Person responsible	Changes needed
B. Program adaptations (*continued*)			

2. Transportation
  a. Vehicles
  b. Parking
  c. Sidewalks
	Begin ASAP; finish in 4 weeks; review with program evaluation	Consultant; representative from The Arc	a. No transportation provided; parents agree to transport for field trips
			b. Parking space by door designated and marked. How many needed?
			c. Sidewalks OK; need curb cut from parking lot

Figure 4. Sample of self-study checklist addressing transportation.

Area	Time line/ Review date	Person responsible	Changes needed
B. Program adaptations (*continued*)			
3. Communication—auxiliary aids and services	Begin ASAP; finish in 2 weeks, review with program evaluation	Program director	3. No students in need of adaptations, aids or services now; have called telephone company for information for future needs; one parent with a visual impairment has made arrangements to call another parent who will read all written materials

Figure 5. Sample of self-study checklist addressing communication.

They also ensure that the organization is in compliance with accepted legal standards.

Policies and procedures should be written as clearly, completely, and concisely as possible while still addressing all the key operations of the organization. To get started, follow these guidelines:

1. Develop a mission statement and philosophy for your program.
2. Collect copies and review all pertinent regulations (e.g., licensing requirements). Remember that these are *minimum* standards.
3. Think about the areas of your program that need to have procedures established to accomplish your mission and meet licensing standards.

An operations manual that contains all the policies and procedures often includes the following topics:

Personnel
    Hiring and recruitment
    Benefits
    Training/staff development
    Evaluation/performance appraisal
    Termination and grievances
    Job descriptions
Finances
    Budget
    Tuition
    Income sources and billing
    Financial aid and scholarships
Programming
    Organizational chart
    Nondiscrimination

Admission, program eligibility, and discharge

Suspected abuse and neglect

Health, medications, injuries, and communicable diseases

Discipline behavior management

Records and confidentiality

Emergency plans—program closing, inclement weather, building evacuation

Food service and nutrition

Parent involvement

Curriculum and educational philosophy

Problem resolution/grievances

There are also other operating procedures that are the "nitty gritty" of the daily program, help the day flow well, and are more easily subject to change (e.g., field trips, co-oping in a classroom, birthday and holiday parties).

Figures 6 and 7 illustrate a center's policy before the Americans with Disabilities Act and a revision made in the policy to reflect a more inclusive admissions policy.

Figure 8 is a sample of how one center explains its toileting policy. Figure 9 is a sample of a formal policy on nutrition that was

---

We welcome all children who are ready to benefit from our program of play and learning. Children should have the skills necessary to enjoy a wide range of activities. Age-appropriate development in the following areas is important: the ability to communicate with others, the ability to play alone and in groups, and the ability to move with coordination.

Our program is based on respect of others and respect for property. Children must be ready to benefit from a group situation.

Children from ages 2½ to 5 years may enroll. All children must be toilet trained.

Figure 6.   Sample admissions policy developed before the Americans with Disabilities Act. (From *Pre-ADA admissions policy of the Falls Church—McLean Children's Center*, Falls Church, VA; reprinted by permission.)

An initial interview with both parents and child is required. Children ages 3–6 years are eligible to attend the center. Our general policy is to expect children to be toilet trained prior to admission. However, the individual needs of each child will be assessed in the initial interview. The interview is a good opportunity for the parents to visit the center, to ask any questions, and to assess the appropriateness of the center for their child. At this time, the parents will receive all necessary forms needed to enroll their child in the center.

Figure 7.   Sample admissions policy developed after the Americans with Disabilities Act. (From *Current admissions policy of the Falls Church—McLean Children's Center*, Falls Church, VA; reprinted by permission.)

We accept into the program children who are not toilet trained and try to reinforce the system of toilet training used at home. We do not attempt to toilet train children independent of parents' efforts. However, younger children who see older children using the toilet often begin to model the older ones' behavior.

Figure 8.   Sample of a statement about toilet training. (From *Current admissions policy of the Falls Church—McLean Children's Center*, Falls Church, VA; reprinted by permission.)

POLICY: The Community Child Care Center shall provide healthy and nutritious snacks and/or meals for all children.

PROCEDURES:
1. Meals and snacks are prepared by a professional catering service under the supervision of a registered dietitian. The cost of the service is included in the weekly tuition.
2. All meals and snacks meet one third of the recommended daily allowance requirements and the provision of hot meals in relation to hours of attendance as required by child care licensing standards.
3. Parents may elect to pack and send lunch for their child. The cost of lunch will be deducted from the weekly tuition.
4. To the extent possible, accommodations for religious or cultural restrictions will be honored with notification from the family or guardian.
5. Parents will be asked about food-related allergies when their child is admitted to the program.
6. Dining areas will be maintained in a pleasant and sanitary manner with the provision of appropriate seating, dishes, and utensils.
7. No snacks or meals will be withheld from a child as a form of punishment.

Figure 9.   Sample policy on nutrition.

written specifically to meet licensing and funding source regulatory requirements.

Many centers also have parent handbooks that contain information about the daily operations of the program. It is helpful for prospective parents and parents of children enrolled in the center to know what the programming and policies of a center are like. Topics in a parent handbook may include the following:

    I. Purpose and organization of the program
       History
       Philosophy/mission statement
       Nondiscrimination statement
       Program description and goals
       Group size and ratios
       Organizational chart/administrative structure
       Funding
       Licensing
   II. Daily operations
       Calendar
       Hours of operation
       Pick-up and drop-off
       Absences
       Parties and graduation
       Classroom rules
       Field trips
       Toilet training
       Nap time
       Mealtime
       What your child should bring to school
  III. Parent involvement
       Communication
       Parent orientation

       Parent conferences
       Parent workshops
  IV. Policies and procedures
       Admissions and withdrawal
          Eligibility
          Enrollment
          Placement
          Suspension, withdrawal, termination
       Tuition and other charges
       Health, illness, injuries, and medicine
       Emergencies
       Discipline
       Records and confidentiality

All of the formal written policies of the program need not be included in the consumer information. An informational and more "user-friendly" version can be adopted. This information should clearly convey the idea that your program does not discriminate against children with disabilities.

For the policy section of the self-study, you should review all your written program materials including policies and procedures, brochures and program information, parent handbook, operating procedures, forms, and job descriptions. If there are aspects of your program that are not documented in writing, start drafting procedures. Carefully review your admission and hiring policies to ensure that they are nondiscriminatory and do not exclude children or job applicants with disabilities. Figure 10 is a sample of a checklist for addressing policies and procedures.

Area	Time line/ Review date	Person responsible	Changes needed
B. Program adaptations (*continued*)			

4. Written materials
  a. Policies and procedures
  b. Brochure/program information
  c. Parent information
  d. Operating procedures
  e. Forms
  f. Other written materials
	Begin ASAP; complete review within 3 months; review annually with program evaluation	Committee: program director, parent, and staff member	a. Policies and procedures complete, reviewed for contradictions to ADA; change policy on toilet training
			b. Write and add nondiscrimination to program information
			c. Add change on toilet training to parent information
			d. Operating procedures reviewed and okayed
			e. Forms reviewed; no changes needed

Figure 10. Sample of self-study checklist addressing policies and procedures

Addressing Your Staff Development Needs You can survey your staff to find out what training and experience they have had related to people with disabilities. Ask what information and support they would like in order to feel more comfortable and knowledgeable. Ask what their concerns and hopes are for this new experience. Make sure that these are addressed when you develop a training plan. Figure 11 is a sample of a checklist for addressing staff development needs.

Figure 12 is a sample training plan that can be generated based on staff needs.

Locating Your Resources Collect information about national, state, and local agencies that can offer you advice, information, and technical assistance on the laws and specific disabilities. Figure 13 is a sample of a checklist for addressing your resources.

The ADA expects programs to aggressively seek out resources to help with the changes needed to include children, families, and employees with disabilities. Having this listing in advance will be a great benefit if you need to use it. Table 1 is a sample resource list.

Area	Time line/ Review date	Person responsible	Changes needed
C. Staff awareness and training			
1. Knowledge 2. Needs 3. Training plan	Begin ASAP; finish in 1 week; review annually	Program director	c. Add section on working with children with disabilities to the current needs assessment for training; administer to staff; develop training plan based on findings

Figure 11. Sample of self-study checklist addressing staff development needs.

Month	Topic/content	Time (in hours)
September	**Values and attitudes about disabilities** Speaker from Disabilities Advocacy Group	2
November	**Disability awareness** Speaker from The Arc	1
January	**Inclusion philosophy** Panel of parents, representatives from special education program, teacher of a child with a disability	2
March	**Understanding special education** Speakers from the public school system	2
May	**Strategies for successful inclusion** Private educational consultant	2
	Total hours	10

Figure 12. Sample of staff training plan.

Area	Time line/ Review date	Person responsible	Changes needed
D. Resources			
1. Disability resources 2. ADA resources	Begin ASAP; ongoing	Program director, with help of staff and parents	Program has current listing of resources; add section on disability-related topics (Can this be put on computer in future?); develop system to add new resources

Figure 13.   Sample of self-study checklist addressing resources.

Your list should include the following information:

- Agency name
- Name of contact person
- Address
- Telephone and fax number
- Services provided

THE COMPLIANCE PLAN

After you finish the self-study, summarize the results and record them. The complete Compliance Checklist (Figure 14) is one example of how to organize the information. Include notations of problems and propose solutions. First, consider solutions that would have no budget impact—in other words, no-cost solutions. For example, increasing your volunteer help through the Foster Grandparents Program or other community agencies can give you extra

Table 1.   Sample resource list

Agency	Contact person	Address	Services
The Arc	Candace Knught	101 Main Street Great Falls, West Virginia	Respite care Information Advocacy
Child Find	Lynne Owens	Public Schools 2100 N. Edmunds Street Romney, West Virginia	Child Find Evaluation Special education and related services
Department of Social Services	Elizabeth White	Office of Child Care 402 W. Broad Street Wheeling, West Virginia	Child care resource and referral State licensing Provider training
State Department of Special Education	Jayne Henry	213 Bank Street Wheeling, West Virginia	Special education
National Information Service for Children and Youth with Disabilities	Ronald Hornbeck	27 N. Rembrandt Boulevard Washington, D.C.	Information Advocacy

Area	Fully met comments	Partially met		Not met	
		Problems	Solutions	Problems	Solutions
A. Physical accessibility					
1. Entrances, hallways, stairways					
2. Other access to goods and services (e.g., classrooms, play spaces, cafeteria, meeting rooms, playground, staff lounge, offices)					
3. Access to restrooms					
4. Other necessary measures					
B. Program adaptations					
1. Classroom					
a. Schedule					
b. Curriculum					
c. Room arrangement					
d. Equipment/materials					
e. Placement/promotion					
2. Transportation					
a. Vehicles					
b. Parking					
c. Sidewalks					
3. Communication—auxiliary aids and services					
4. Written materials					
a. Policies and procedures					
b. Brochure/program information					
c. Parent information					
d. Operating procedures					
e. Forms					
f. Other written materials					
C. Staff awareness and training					
1. Knowledge					
2. Needs					
3. Training plan					
D. Resources					
1. Disability resources					
2. ADA resources					

Figure 14. Compliance Checklist and corrective action plan.

hands in the classroom. A local university or community college may be able to provide speakers for your staff development programs. Although there are time, effort, and planning costs on the part of the children, families, and staff, many creative solutions will have little budget impact.

Next, organize other solutions into low-cost and costly categories. The format of the Compliance Checklist is similar to the one required for the National Association for the Education of Young Children (NAEYC) accreditation. If you are pursuing accreditation, you already are involved in a self-study of your program. In this case, complying with the ADA simply can become one more piece of the process.

The next sections give examples of some common problems and a variety of solutions for use in the compliance plan. The format of the compliance plan parallels the format of the self-study.

Addressing Physical
Accessibility Problems in the Classroom

Problem: The program has classrooms on two floors with a standard stairway.

No-cost solutions

- Move the classroom of a child with a physical disability from the second floor to a ground level room so it is accessible.
- If the parent of a child has difficulty walking or uses a wheelchair, make arrangements for a staff person to meet the child at the car.

Low-cost solutions

- If practical, obtain a portable folding ramp that can be transported and used in many places.

Costly solutions

- Consult with building contractors and equipment suppliers to estimate costs of proposed modifications, such as building ramps or widening doorways. Sometimes physical alteration is the only acceptable solution. Remember that any new construction must meet ADA accessibility guidelines before it is built.

Addressing Program
Accessibility Problems in the Classroom

Problem: A young child is not as independent as his or her peers and wanders out of the classroom.

No-cost solutions

- Talk to other teachers about older students who could assist as tutors in activities that are difficult for this child.
- Try to locate classroom volunteers to assist all the students.

Low-cost solutions

- Ask if a simple latch can be installed on the classroom door, out of the children's reach.
- Look for special education consultants in your community who would be available for assistance when the need arises to make changes in your programming.

Costly solutions

- Hire a teaching assistant to assist with all the children so the child who wanders can be watched easily.

Addressing Program
Accessibility Problems with Transportation

Problem: Transportation is needed to attend the program.

No-cost solutions

• A family or employee voluntarily provides his or her own transportation.

Low-cost solutions

• See if there are volunteer organizations in your community that can assist with transportation.
• See if the child or adult in need of transportation is entitled to transportation or assistance with the cost of transportation as part of his or her personal benefits.
• Adapt an existing van by buying a portable ramp, removing a seat, and installing a wheelchair tie-down.

Costly solutions

• Buy a van with a lift.
• Make arrangements for hiring special transportation.

Addressing Program
Accessibility Problems with Communication

Problem: A parent or employee has a hearing impairment and does not use a standard telephone.

No-cost solutions

• If parents or employees have hearing impairments, make sure that all communications are written for them.

Low-cost solutions

• Locate professionals in your community who are available for sign interpretation.
• Investigate the cost of relay service through your local telephone company.

Costly solutions

• Purchase a telecommunication device for people with hearing impairments.

Each state has relay telecommunications services for individuals with speech and hearing impairments. Anyone using a standard telephone who wishes to "talk" to an individual who has a speech or hearing impairment calls an operator. The call and conversation is relayed both ways by a special operator with a telecommunication device. Contact your local telephone company or AT&T at 1-800-855-1155 to get information. States also may have a telecommunication assistance program that assists in paying for and obtaining auxiliary aids and devices, such as a TDD. You may not have an immediate need for additional equipment, but keep a list of resources.

Addressing Program Accessibility Problems with Written Materials

Problem: Your program policies and procedures need revision to comply with the Americans with Disabilities Act.

No-cost solutions

- Adopt materials from other programs that already have been developed and are in compliance with the ADA.

Low-cost solutions

- Write amendments and add them to the materials.

Costly solutions

- Rewrite and publish all program materials to reflect the new philosophy.

Addressing Program Accessibility Problems with Staff Training

Problem: Staff request information about the ADA and inclusion.

No-cost solutions

- Locate local resources that can provide in-service training at no cost. Therapists and parents of children with disabilities often are willing to help train staff. Universities and community colleges may be good sources of instructors.

Low-cost solutions

- Write a grant to support training for your staff.
- Find local funding for in-service training from a professional organization or philanthropist.

Costly solutions

- Hire consultants to provide training.
- Budget money to support staff development provided at local colleges, universities, and professional conferences.

Addressing Program Accessibility Problems with Resources

Problem: Need to find people to answer questions about the ADA and provide guidance and information about the laws and about children with disabilities.

No-cost solutions

- Search for local resources (e.g., administrators of inclusive programs, lawyers who specialize in disability law) to support children with disabilities.

- Call disability organizations such as United Cerebral Palsy Association, Inc. and The Arc for free publications and materials.

Low-cost solutions

- Purchase materials and resources that provide information about supporting children with disabilities.

Costly solutions

- Allocate money in budget to hire consultants to advise staff about including children with disabilities.

This is only a sample of concerns and potential solutions. Administrators should try to network with other program administrators who have similar concerns. Inquire at professional meetings how other centers are making program changes. Talk to staff, parents, and governing boards to brainstorm about solutions to address each of the identified problem areas. Seek the help of the Child Care Law Center and the ADA technical assistance office in your region.

Set Priorities for Making Changes

If you need help understanding federal, state, or local requirements, contact your regional Technical Assistance Center at 1-800-949-4232 (Voice and TDD). Making your program as physically accessible as possible should be a top priority. Remember, any new construction and many alterations must meet accessibility guidelines. Written materials, such as policies and procedures, program descriptions, brochures, parent handbooks, and staff training, usually are revised regularly, so you can incorporate needed revisions about serving children with disabilities during that process. You should consider a range of program changes and accommodations that might be needed if a child with a disability is enrolled. Think of possible situations and develop a process you can use to make the modifications. Be ready to make necessary changes as the need arises. Decide which solutions best address the identified problems. Prioritize the list of solutions and make a schedule for completing the changes. Designate the person responsible for each task.

Complete the options that have little or no cost These may seem the simplest solutions to implement. However, it is still important to assign these tasks and follow up on their completion.
Budget for and make low-cost adaptations and accommodations Completing some of these solutions may require a review of the budget to see if funds are available. It may necessitate reallocating previously designated funds or seeking new money.
Consider and plan for alterations, renovations, and purchases that would involve greater cost These changes will involve seeking new funding; some of the changes will need to wait until funding can be found. Do not forget to take advantage of any tax credits that your organization is eligible for. Document what

you would do if funding were available. Clearly state the changes where costs exceed the financial capability of your program.

Document Your Efforts

Keep your self-study notes, records of completed work, and plans for compliance on file. Although the law does not require a self-study or compliance plan, you now have written documentation showing that you have given careful consideration to adjusting your program to accommodate children, family members, and employees with disabilities.

FOLLOW UP ON PROPOSED CHANGES ANNUALLY

Once you have completed the self-study, it is very important to follow through and make the changes required. During the first year, the implementation should be monitored frequently to document progress and make revisions if new barriers are encountered. Circumstances may arise that necessitate new considerations or revisions to previously made plans. After the compliance plan has been completed, review it annually to reevaluate whether more or different improvements are readily achievable. Examine the changes that you have made in the past year in each of the self-study areas and see if additional ones are needed. Add your ADA compliance plan to your program evaluation and update it on a regular basis.

Although the program change process outlined here may not be feasible for every program, it provides a framework to begin thinking about possible changes and gives some suggestions about how to make changes. It is important to start today to think about how and what might be needed to accommodate the next child seeking admission. Most of these changes are good for all children, not just children with disabilities.

Appendix

Changes within the Classroom and Playground

The following photographs are of classroom and playground equipment that can be seen at typical child care centers. The questions next to the photographs are representative of ones that can be asked when assessing accessibility issues at your center.

These steps lead to the playground. Can all children get to the playground? What if a child cannot see, walk well, or climb stairs?

These swings are typical of those found on playgrounds at child care centers. Can all children use them? What about children with balance problems or who cannot sit well?

The coat rack is very accessible. But can the hooks be adjusted so that all children, including children using wheelchairs, can reach them?

The way in which the furniture is arranged does not appear to provide enough room for a child using a wheelchair to maneuver. If the furniture is rearranged, how will the child with a visual impairment know where things are?

Can a child with mobility problems get to the loft? Is a child who is unable to see safe at the top?

The sandbox appears to provide children with much enjoyment. But is it accessible to all children? Can a child get to the sandbox if he or she uses a wheelchair?

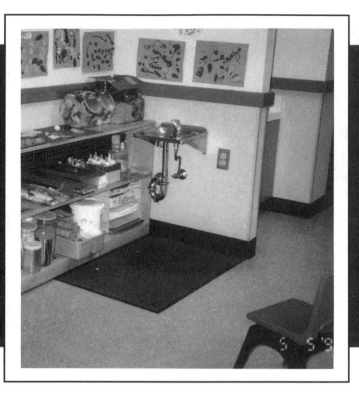

A child using a wheelchair can fit under this drinking fountain, but how can the lever or button be operated to get a drink?

The bathroom stall is very small for a wheelchair to fit. If a child uses a wheelchair, is there enough space for him or her to reach the toilet and someone to help? If a child has poor sitting balance, is this a safe bathroom?

This is an example of a swing with sides that lower to the ground. A wheelchair can be pushed up and the sides raised. Both child and the wheelchair swing.

The drinking fountain has a recessed space to accommodate a wheelchair and has a simple push panel to operate the water. Any child can easily get a drink of water.

6

Welcoming Families to Your Center

First impressions are important. When a parent calls to ask about your center and makes an appointment to visit, it is the first step in building a new relationship. Parents are your most important allies as you work to meet the needs of each child in your program. If you can communicate with them, your job is easier and the child benefits. If communication is strained for any reason, your work on behalf of the child is more complicated. This relationship is especially crucial when a child has a disability because parents are your primary source of information about the child.

PARENTS ARE INDIVIDUALS

The first rule to remember is that parents are as diverse and unique as their children. Do not assume that a parent's behavior is a reaction to the presence of a disability in their child. In most ways parents of children with disabilities are just like other parents. They may be easy to approach and ready to talk about their children or they may be reticent and reluctant to share personal information.

An important difference is that parents of a child with a disability are more likely to have experienced situations in which their child was rejected or not welcomed. Some parents may arrive on your doorstep angry, defensive, and demanding because of these past experiences. They may be extremely sensitive to questions about their child and have the expectation that your response to their inquiries also will be negative. If you can appreciate how hurtful these past rejections were, you can prepare to respond supportively.

Other parents may be reluctant to discuss their child's disability openly. They may be afraid that if you have all the facts about the disability, you will not want their child in your center. They also may think that your concern about the disability will lead you to judge their child by the disability and treat him or her differently. Again, your supportive responses and sensitive questions can put parents' concerns to rest.

One mother responded, *"I didn't want to tell the preschool that Michael had cerebral palsy. I was afraid they would coddle him and not expect him to be able to do things as well as the other children. I didn't want Michael to be pre-judged; I just wanted him to be treated like a regular kid."*

Another parent echoed these feelings, *"The first three centers I called told me they wouldn't take Carla because of her cleft palate. When I called the fourth center, I was angry. I told them that Carla had a disability and they better accept her or I would sue them. I know that's not a good beginning but I felt so helpless. I just wanted to find a place that would give Carla a chance."*

And in a third case, one caregiver stated, *"When I called a child care center and inquired about enrolling Eddie, the director was very encouraging. I felt it was only fair to tell her that he is receiving special education services. There was a big pause and she asked, 'How handicapped is your child?' I immediately wondered how much I should tell her because I was afraid she would say that the center didn't work with children with this type of disability."*

When parents or caregivers have experiences such as these, they can understandably become very apprehensive about calling centers to find care for their children.

INITIAL CONTACT

The first contact with a parent is often by telephone. In this first conversation, try to gather only preliminary information such as parents' names, child's name and age, address, and telephone numbers. It is probably best to avoid discussing personal information at this time. Instead, briefly describe your program so that parents have some idea of your hours, the ages of children served, and the cost. You also can set up time for a tour. This first contact is an opportunity to set a positive tone. By 1) giving clear information about the program, 2) setting up a convenient time for a tour, and 3) letting parents decide how much information to share about their child, you are helping parents feel in control and laying the groundwork for a positive relationship.

Try to approach each initial contact with an open mind. When parents start to describe their child's disabilities you may begin to worry about whether you can meet all those needs. Can your staff provide an appropriate program for the child? Does the child have extensive needs that will require special equipment or expensive adaptations? Will staff and other families have questions and concerns about the child's presence?

As your list of concerns grows write them down, but do not voice them to the parents yet. At this first stage, you and the parents are just getting to know each other. They are evaluating you and your center and trying to decide if their child will be welcomed.

You will have plenty of time to discuss your concerns if the parents decide to enroll. Right now you want to put them at ease and begin to gather information. Your goal is to communicate your willingness to discuss the issues and work together to find ways to meet both their needs and your program's needs.

When parents call your center, remember what they are looking for. First, they want to know if your program will be a good place for their child. As you talk, they may be asking themselves these questions:

- Will my child be safe?
- Will the people here like and accept my child?
- Will my child make friends and be happy?
- How will my child get along here?
- Will my child learn new skills?

Parents need information to decide if your program is right for them and their child. Specifically, they need to know about

- Location
- Program cost
- Program philosophy
- Program hours
- Group size
- Child–staff ratios
- Curriculum
- Staff experience
- Registration procedures

Parents of a child with a disability also may be interested in your center's physical accessibility, the training and experience your staff has had with children with disabilities, and the availability of special education or other therapeutic services.

THE FIRST MEETING: GETTING MORE INFORMATION

When parents come to visit your center, this may be the first face-to-face meeting. It is a time for parents to see the center and for you to gather more in-depth information about what they want and what their child needs. This first visit might include the following steps:

1. Tour the center first.
2. Find out if the parents wish to pursue enrollment.
3. Finish giving them information and answering their questions about the program in a quiet area.
4. Ask them to describe their child in more detail and find out what type of program they are seeking for their child.
5. Talk about the match between what your program provides and what they are seeking for their child. If you have concerns about

the match, now is the time to voice your concerns, but do it honestly and sensitively. Put yourself in the parents' place—how would you like to be treated in a similar situation?

6. Explain clearly and carefully the enrollment procedures including all fees.

Remember that you should not ask directly about the presence of a disability. If a parent offers this information, it may be included in the discussion about the type of program that the parents are seeking for their child. This is one way that you can get information about what special needs the parents expect your center to meet.

Ask only for the information you *need to know* to make the best possible admission/placement decision. Respect the parents' right and the child's right to privacy. If you need to press for further information, explain how and why it would be helpful to know more about the child and his or her needs. Ask about the child's current program and services. Find out if people currently working with the child would be a helpful resource.

How to Ask for Needed Information

Open-ended questions or comments are nonjudgmental ways to gather the information you need. One way to communicate your openness is to use "person-first" language. Always put the child before the disability. For example, rather than saying "your Down syndrome child" you would refer to "your child with Down syndrome." "Person-first" language is discussed more fully in Chapter 10. Put yourself in the parents' place and think about how you would feel being asked the following questions:

Nonjudgmental: "Tell me about your child."
Accusatory: "What's wrong with your child?"
Neutral: "Does your child have a specific diagnosis?"
Intrusive: "How disabled is your child?"

Remember that knowing the diagnosis may be little help in deciding how to meet a child's needs. It is more important to learn about who the child is by finding out what he likes, how he plays, and how he communicates. When any child comes to your program it is important to gather some developmental background information that would help you provide the best services for the child. For all children, consider using an information-gathering sheet such as the Child Profile (see Chapter 11, Figure 2) and the accompanying questions to guide this conversation.

Give It Time

A positive relationship with the parents is in your best interest whether or not the child ever enrolls in your program. If you reject a child because she has a disability and you are worried about caring for her, you risk angering parents who may decide to file a discrimination complaint or talk poorly of your center to others.

If you are concerned that you will not be able to accommodate a child, give the parents some specific information about how your program operates. Describe the class size, the ratios, and some typical activities. Talk about the amount of time and supervision that staff can provide each child. This information will help parents decide if your center is right for their child.

Feel free to talk about your experience or lack of experience serving children with disabilities. If your staff has not had special training, let the parents know. If you have never enrolled a child in a wheelchair, say so. At the same time, you should communicate your willingness to try new approaches.

Even if your main concern is cost, try not to rush into a discussion of what changes you can and cannot afford to make. Keep reminding yourself that these conversations are just a beginning. An unanticipated solution may present itself if you keep an open mind.

The following cases are examples of initial encounters between families and child care centers that illustrate how important good communication can be.

A Rough Start

◄○► ◄○► ◄○►

Vivian Baldwin, the director of Wee Ones Child Development Center, got a call from Ms. Gordon who was looking for a program for her 3-year-old son Ian. Vivian told Ms. Gordon that there was one space available in the young 3s group and invited Ms. Gordon to visit. They made an appointment for later that afternoon.

Ms. Gordon toured the center and then met with Vivian. Vivian answered questions about the program and asked if she felt the program would meet Ian's needs. At that point, Ms. Gordon told her that Ian had spina bifida, wore braces, and used a walker. She liked the center, wanted to enroll him, and hoped that Ian could start Monday.

Vivian was speechless. She had never met a child with spina bifida and had no idea what this might mean for her program. She told Ms. Gordon that she didn't know if the program could meet Ian's needs.

Ms. Gordon was adamant. She told Vivian that according to the Americans with Disabilities Act the center had to accept Ian.

Vivian hesitated. She didn't know how Ian would get up and down stairs or whether he would be able to use the playground, and she worried about how her staff would cope. She told Ms. Gordon that Wee Ones wasn't accessible and couldn't afford to install an elevator or a ramp.

Ms. Gordon became angry. She told Vivian that she wouldn't send Ian where he wasn't wanted and she made it clear that Vivian would be hearing from her attorney.

Now Vivian was angry. She felt that Ms. Gordon was threatening her and she honestly believed that Wee Ones would not be a good place for Ian. She showed Ms. Gordon out and suggested that she find a program where the staff had training to work with children like Ian.

◄●► ◄●► ◄●►

This exchange was unfortunate for both Vivian and Ms. Gordon. Vivian was surprised and unprepared for Ms. Gordon's disclosure about Ian. Ms. Gordon was defensive and quick to take offense at any hint of rejection. The conversation quickly deteriorated and both parties felt hurt and mistreated at the end.

To avoid such situations in the future, Vivian could ask parents to bring their child to the center for a visit as part of the enrollment process prior to deciding on group placement. This way the staff members could get to know each child before the child was assigned to a group.

Vivian also could invite parents to let her know if their child has any special needs so that the center can plan for those needs. If a parent disclosed unexpected information about his or her child, Vivian could express her surprise and suggest setting up a conference to discuss the child and his or her programming needs in depth. This might avoid an angry confrontation.

A Good Beginning

◄●► ◄●► ◄●►

Mrs. Rogers visited the Woodlawn Montessori Center on Monday morning unannounced. Mr. Cooper, the director, greeted her and offered to give her a tour of the center.

During the tour Mr. Cooper found out that Mrs. Rogers was looking for a program for her daughter Samantha who was almost 3 years old. Mr. Cooper had an opening in the right group, and Mrs. Rogers spent some time observing that class.

After the tour, Mrs. Rogers said that she liked the program and wanted to enroll Samantha so she could start the following week. Mr. Cooper wanted to find out more about Samantha and asked if she was in a program now. Mrs. Rogers hesitated and then said that Samantha went to a special education program three mornings a week. She had been a late walker and wasn't talking yet.

Mr. Cooper suggested that Mrs. Rogers bring Samantha to visit and asked what Mrs. Rogers hoped that Woodlawn would be able to offer. Mrs. Rogers said she could bring Samantha the next day. She said she wanted Samantha to be with children her own age who were talking and Woodlawn looked just right.

Mr. Cooper explained that neither he nor his teachers had much experience with children who were 3 and not talking. He explained that all children were enrolled on a 1-month trial basis. He would enroll Samantha on the same basis but asked if a few additional meetings could be arranged. Would it be all right with Mrs. Rogers if Samantha's special education teacher visited Woodlawn and helped them understand how best to help Samantha? Mrs. Rogers agreed and offered to set up a meeting with Samantha's special education teacher, her speech-language therapist, and the staff at Woodlawn. She also suggested that Mr. Cooper and Samantha's new teacher visit the special education program.

Mr. Cooper then described how the classes at Woodlawn operated. He told Mrs. Rogers that there were 16 children ages 2½–4 years in the class with two teachers. He explained how the children worked independently alone and in small groups. He wanted to be sure that Mrs. Rogers understood that the teachers' role was to guide and support the children in choosing learning activities rather than teach them through drill and structured group activities.

The next day Mrs. Rogers brought Samantha to visit. Samantha spent some time in the classroom. As Mr. Cooper watched, Samantha dumped the toys on the floor and moved quickly around the room. She snatched a puzzle from one child and put the pieces in her mouth. Mr. Cooper was worried. He told Mrs. Rogers that he wasn't sure if Woodlawn was the best place for Samantha.

Mrs. Rogers was quite determined. She explained that it takes some time for Samantha to adjust. She offered to start her for half a day and stay with her for the first few days. She suggested meeting with Mr. Cooper and the teacher at the end of 2 weeks to discuss the situation. If things were not improving, they could consider what should be done next.

Mr. Cooper was relieved. He felt that Mrs. Rogers understood his concerns and was reassured by her offer to set up a meeting with the specialists and help out in the classroom.

◄○► ◄○► ◄○►

Mr. Cooper is on his way to building a positive relationship with Mrs. Rogers. The situation is still fragile because Mr. Cooper has doubts about Woodlawn's ability to meet Samantha's needs, but Mrs. Rogers is determined that Samantha be given an opportunity to succeed.

Consulting with Samantha's special education teacher and speech-language therapist are good first steps. They will be able to help Woodlawn make appropriate changes and develop reasonable expectations for Samantha.

Starting gradually and setting up regular meetings also are sound ideas. Not all families are able to start part time and help out in the classroom. But it is helpful to schedule regular times to talk during the adjustment period.

QUESTIONS TO KEEP IN MIND

The following list of questions can remind you of the concerns to address when a parent of a child with special needs calls your program:

1. Have I conveyed a program philosophy that is accepting and flexible?
2. Have I clearly communicated important program information?
3. Have I gathered the necessary information about the family's wishes and the child's needs in a nonjudgmental and supportive manner?
4. Have I openly discussed expectations about enrollment and placement?
5. Have we agreed upon and scheduled the next step in the process?
6. Have I set a positive tone for future conversations?

These are only the first steps. Building a relationship takes time. As the parents get to know and trust you and your staff, this relationship will strengthen. Open and frequent communication is the key to this process.

Understanding
Special Education Services

Chapter 1 described the laws related to the Americans with Disabilities Act that were historical precedents and that ensured people with disabilities civil rights and education. Many children are eligible for and receive special education services through their public school system. You can gain access to resources for children in your program by understanding your state and local special education laws and how they work in your community. See the Resources at the back of this book for information about how to obtain a fact sheet listing state agencies and resources for people with disabilities.

CHILD-FIND SERVICES

One of the services provided by all local school systems is *Child Find* for young children. Child Find is the service that identifies young children with disabilities and helps them obtain special education services, if they qualify. All states are charged with having procedures ensuring that

> all children residing in the State who are disabled, regardless of the severity of their disability, and who are in need of special education and related services are identified, located, and evaluated, and that a practical method is developed and implemented to determine which children are currently receiving needed special education and related services and which children are not currently receiving needed special education and related services. (PL 102-119, Sec. 1412, [2][C])

Parents who have a child, age 3–5 (younger children may be eligible, depending on state and local regulations), can contact Child Find in the special education division of their local public school system if they have concerns about their child's development. Look in the local telephone directory for the local public school system of the child. Call the general information number or the special education services number to get the Child Find listing. It will provide screening and assessment at no cost for children who may have a disability and be in need of special education services. When you suspect that a child has special learning needs, refer the parents to Child Find for an assessment. Anyone can make a referral to Child Find, but parents or guardians must give permission for any testing and evaluation. Parents also have the option of seeking a private evaluation.

◄o► ◄o► ◄o►

Sheryl, a teacher at the Pooh Bear Children's Center, was preparing for parent conferences. She was worried about Chi, one of her 3-year-olds, and wanted to discuss her concerns with Chi's parents. Chi said only a few words and those were unclear—compared to the other children in the class, her speech skills were delayed. The director of the center, Ms. Duncan, helped Sheryl by making telephone calls to find an appropriate place where Chi could be evaluated. She called the local school system because she had seen a small advertisement in the local paper offering free screening and assessment if parents were concerned about their child's development. This turned out to be the Child Find office. The person at Child Find explained the screening and evaluation services offered and said she would send Ms. Duncan flyers for all her parents. She told Ms. Duncan to have Chi's parents call to set up an appointment. Ms. Duncan was pleased to hear that there would be no cost for any of these services.

When Sheryl heard about the Child-Find services, she knew this was what Chi needed. In her meeting with Chi's parents, she explained her concerns and gave them the information about Child Find. Chi's parents were upset by the prospect that their child might have some developmental delays, but everyone felt better knowing that help was available.

◄o► ◄o► ◄o►

Evaluation

If parents decide to seek an evaluation through Child-Find services, they need to call and make an appointment. They will be asked to give written permission for the testing. They also will be asked to fill out forms giving information about their child. They may be asked to sign a release to obtain information from other sources, such as hospitals or doctors. As the child's current teacher you also have valuable information that can help in the evaluation of the child. You may be asked to provide written information about the child such as a report describing the child and detailing your concerns.

Special education laws provide specific due process procedures and protections to parents. As they begin the assessment process, they are protected by specific rights. Parents must give written permission before their child can be evaluated and testing must be conducted in the child's native language if necessary. Parents also may request that any conferences be held in their native language. Parents have the right to know what types of assessment will be done, the length of the assessments, and how long it will take to get the results. A full evaluation is conducted by a multidisciplinary team that includes a teacher and at least one other specialist who is knowledgeable about the suspected area of disability. This multidisciplinary team also can include a psychologist, a special educator, and other service providers, such as occupational, physical, and speech-language therapists. Any test given must be free of racial or cultural bias. Parents have the right to seek an independent evaluation if they disagree with the results of the testing.

Parents should be given information about the process that will follow the evaluation. After the testing is complete, an eligibility meeting will be held to determine if their child will be found eligible or ineligible for special education services. If their child is eligible, the parents and the multidisciplinary team write a plan to guide the provision of education and related services. This plan is called an individualized family service plan (IFSP) or an individualized education program (IEP). After the plan is written, the parents and personnel from the school system decide what classroom or placement would best provide the services that are needed. The services must begin according to the time line determined by federal law and state guidelines. This is usually within 45 days of the determination of eligibility. A child eligible for special education services must be provided those services free of charge in a public program.

◄o► ◄o► ◄o►

Chi's mother called Sheryl to let her know that she had taken Chi for an assessment and that Chi was found eligible for speech-language services provided by the school system. There was going to be a meeting to develop an individualized education program, and Chi's mother had been encouraged to invite other interested people, particularly Chi's current teacher. When Sheryl went to the meeting she learned about the assessment findings and was asked to help develop speech and language goals based on her experience with Chi at the Pooh Bear Children's Center. The children at the center were given lots of choices for activities, but Chi never expressed what she wanted to do. Sheryl suggested that Chi work on learning to make choices, first by pointing and then by using words. Although Chi's speech-language therapy was scheduled at the public school in the mornings before she went to Pooh Bear, the speech-language therapist wanted to make sure that everyone worked on the same language goals, both at home and in the child care program.

◄o► ◄o► ◄o►

THE INDIVIDUALIZED FAMILY SERVICE PLAN
OR THE INDIVIDUALIZED EDUCATION PROGRAM

When a child is found to be eligible for early intervention or special education services, a meeting is held and a plan specifying learning goals and special education services is written. An IFSP is for children from birth through age 2, and an IEP is for children ages 3–5. The requirements for these plans were originally defined in PL 94-142, the Education for All Handicapped Children Act of 1975, and PL 99-457, the Education of the Handicapped Act Amendments of 1986, Part H, respectively. The meeting should be scheduled at a time convenient to the parents.

An IFSP meeting should include the parents or guardian, anyone invited by the parents, the service coordinator, and service providers. The people at the meeting review all of the available information about the child and develop appropriate learning goals or outcomes. The IFSP specifies the learning goals, how progress toward the goals will be measured, and when services will begin and end. The IFSP must include the following components:

- A statement of the infant's or toddler's present levels of development (physical, cognitive, speech-language, psychosocial, motor, and self-help)
- A statement of the family's strengths and needs related to the child's development
- A statement of major outcomes expected to be achieved for the child and the family through early intervention
- The criteria, procedures, and time lines for determining progress
- The specific early intervention services necessary to meet the unique needs of the child and family, including the frequency, intensity, and method of delivering services
- The projected dates for the initiation of services and expected duration of those services
- The name of the service coordinator
- The procedures for transition from early intervention into the preschool program

There are no standard forms for the IFSP. The information listed above should be included and the family members should be very involved in deciding what type of program they would like for their child. Figures 1 and 2 are examples of an IFSP.

The public school system usually provides special education and related services to eligible children between the ages of 3 and 21. When a child is found eligible for services, a meeting is held within 30 calendar days to share information about the child and develop a plan that will guide and document the provision of all special education services. An IEP meeting should include the parents or guardian; the child's teacher(s); an administrative representative of the school other than the child's teacher; other individuals, at the discretion of the school or the parents, such as the evaluators;

Early Intervention Program

8472 N. Belmont Street
Arlington, Virginia 22207
(703) 879-6311

Name: Jennifer Winston   **Birthdate:** 7/24/93

Address: 7892 Madison Street
            Arlington, Virginia 22076

Phone: (703) 265-8924

Service Coordinator (Case Manager): Jessica Smithers, MSW

IFSP Team Members and Signatures:

Theresa Winston, mother   _____
Annette Walton, grandmother   _____
Jessica Smithers, social worker _____
Elaine Paxton, nurse   _____
Jane Nessbaum, physical therapist _____
Francis Gallagher, teacher   _____

Frequency, Intensity, and Duration of Services:

Services will begin with the signing of the plan and continue until _Jennifer_ is eligible for public school services (on her second birthday) or when the team feels she is no longer in need of services. Frequency and intensity of services is specified with each written outcome.

IFSP Review Dates: 6/13/95, 12/13/95, 6/13/96

Transition Plan: ___x___ **Not applicable** _____ **Yes, see attached**

Parent Signature(s):

This plan represents my (our) wishes. I (we) understand and agree with it, and I (we) authorize this agency or others designated in the plan to carry it out with me (us).

Signature: _____ **Date:** _____

Figure 1.   Page 1 of a sample individualized family service plan (IFSP).

and the child, when appropriate. An IEP must include the following components:

- A statement of the child's current educational performance levels
- A statement of annual goals and short-term objectives
- A description of the specific special education and related services to be provided

Individualized Family Service Plan

Name: Jennifer Winston

Birthdate: 7/24/93   **Age:** 8 months

Developmental Levels:

Cognitive	6–8 months
Social	6–8 months
Language	6–8 months
Motor	3–4 months

Child's Strengths and Needs:

Jennifer likes to be held and talked to. She enjoys being with people and vocalizes to them. Her mother reports that Jennifer feels like a "rag doll" when held and is a "dead weight" to carry. The therapist reports that Jennifer has low muscle tone and cannot hold her head steady.

Family Resources and Concerns:

Ms. Winston is a single parent and has the help of her mother for child care in the late afternoon. Her employer is understanding, but she needs to work a regular schedule to keep her job because she took so much leave when Jennifer was born. She has found a family home provider for the mornings with the assistance of her social worker. Ms. Winston is worried about getting Jennifer the therapy that she needs and paying for it. Ms. Winston also is worried about the fact that Jennifer does not seem to be gaining weight.

Outcomes:

1. Jennifer will receive physical therapy service on a regular basis for the next 6 months so that she can get physically stronger, sit more easily, and be carried more easily.
2. With the pediatrician's permission, a nutritionist will be consulted to work with Ms. Winston to help Jennifer gain weight appropriately.

Strategies and Activities:

1. a. Home-based physical therapy services will be arranged for Jennifer in the late afternoon, so that she will be rested after her nap and her grandmother can participate in the therapy with her. The therapist will stay in touch with Ms. Winston by phone.
   b. The therapist will make a visit to Jennifer's family home provider to demonstrate handling and positioning and answer questions.
   c. The service coordinator will assist Ms. Winston in the application process for Supplemental Security Income (SSI) through Social Security.
2. a. If the pediatrician has given his permission, the service coordinator will seek referral sources for nutrition services for Jennifer.

Criteria and Time Lines:

1. a. Physical therapy services will begin next week on Tuesday afternoon. A yearly schedule will be decided at that time. Ms. Winston and the therapist will review Jennifer's progress every 6 weeks.
   b. Ms. Winston will complete the SSI forms. She will make a visit to the SSI office with the service coordinator in 3 weeks.
2. a. The service coordinator will call Ms. Winston as soon as she finds out about nutrition resources. In the meantime, Ms. Winston will keep a record of what Jennifer eats for a week. Jennifer weighs 13 pounds now. The pediatrician weighs Jennifer every month so there will be a record of weight loss and gain.

Figure 2.   Page 2 of a sample IFSP.

- A statement of the extent to which the child will be able to participate in regular education programs
- The date on which services will begin and their anticipated duration
- Appropriate objective evaluation criteria and evaluation procedures and schedules for determining, at least annually, whether the short-term objectives are being achieved
- A statement of need for technology devices or services, if appropriate

At this meeting alternatives for placement, including community options, may be considered and discussed to determine which is or are the most appropriate. A parent must give written consent before a child is placed in a special education program. Figures 3–5 are examples of an IEP.

Collaboration with Your Public School System

Your local school system can be an important source of information and support as you include children with disabilities in your program. When a child in your program is found eligible for special education services, you may ask to participate in IEP or IFSP meetings and obtain copies of the documents with the parents' permission. The information in the IEP can guide your curriculum and help you adapt activities to meet the child's needs. If a child attends both a special education program and a community child care program, it is extremely important that staff from both programs communicate with each other regularly so that educational expectations can be coordinated. This can be done through telephone contacts or face-to-face meetings. Another strategy is to start a communication notebook that the child carries in a bookbag. Parents, teachers, and therapists can make entries in the notebook about daily activities, and they can ask and answer questions. This way everyone can stay informed about the child's progress.

Special Education and Related Services

Both the IFSP and IEP must outline the kinds of services that the child is to receive based on that child's needs. The following is a list and short description of the most frequently encountered services.

Special Education or Early Intervention Services Special education is specially designed instruction that meets the child's unique needs and is provided at no cost to the parents. These services usually are provided by someone who has been trained in special education. Using the IEP or IFSP, the special educator develops specific learning activities to enhance the child's learning and minimize the impact of any disabling condition. The special education teacher also collects data to monitor the child's progress. The educator also makes suggestions for adapting the regular curriculum to meet the child's learning needs. Special education services can be provided in a classroom, home, hospital, or other setting. Special education also includes related services.

Medford County Public Schools
Department of Student Services and Special Education

Individualized Education Program

Name: William Student   **ID NO:** 220-76-3848   **Birthdate:** 12/25/90

Parent/Guardian: John and Jill Student   **Phone:** 999-1234

Address: 321 Somewhere Lane, Medford, Virginia 22030

School: Martin Luther King, Jr. Elementary School

Eligibility Date: 6/27/93   **IEP Date:** 8/27/93   **Annual IEP Due:** 8/27/94

Signature of persons present   **Relationship to student**

_____   mother _____

_____   school psychologist _____

_____   teacher _____

_____   speech therapist _____

_____   _____

The IEP Team Recommendation for Placement Is:

Medford County noncategorical preschool program in Martin Luther King, Jr. Elementary School in A.M., Medford County Child Development Center in P.M.

This is agreed to be the least restrictive environment.

_x_ I AGREE or ___ I DO NOT AGREE with the contents of the proposed IEP and with the IEP team recommendation described above. I have been informed of my due process rights both orally and in writing. I understand that I have the right to review my child's records at any time. I understand that the granting of consent is voluntary and may be revoked at any time. I HAVE _x_ /HAVE NOT ___ participated in the development of my child's IEP.

Signature: _____   **Date:** _____

Figure 3.   Page 1 of a sample individualized education program (IEP).

Related Services Related services are transportation and developmental, corrective, and other support services required to assist a child with a disability to benefit from special education. Whether a child receives these services depends on what the child needs. The special education laws include a listing of some services to help a child benefit from special education, such as the following:

- Audiology
- Psychological services
- Medical services for diagnostic or evaluation purposes only
- School health services

Individualized Education Program
page 2

Name: William Student   **School:** Martin Luther King, Jr. E.S.
Primary Disability: Developmental delay
Primary Special Education Placement: Noncategorical preschool
Physical Education Is Provided: Adapted PE with class
Participation in General Education: 25% lunch and recess

Additional Related Services:
Speech Therapy
Small Group Instruction and Consultation
Twice a week, 20- to 30-minute sessions

Description of Student's Current Level of Functioning:
William is 3 years old. His testing indicates that he is delayed in all developmental areas by approximately 6 months with the exception of motor skills that are age-appropriate. He has articulation difficulties and evidence of language processing problems. See assessment reports for details.

Signature: _____   **Date:** _____

Figure 4.   Page 2 of a sample IEP.

- Recreation, including therapeutic recreation
- Counseling services
- Early identification and assessment of disabilities
- Social work
- Parent counseling and training

Three of the most common related services are described below.

Speech-Language Services   Speech-language services are provided by a speech-language pathologist who specializes in communication disorders such as voice quality, pronunciation (articulation), oral motor skills, vocabulary (language), and hearing. Oral motor skills refer to the way the muscles of the mouth and face work. Speech-language therapy helps a child develop and use language. A speech-language therapist also can help develop an augmentative and alternative communication system for children who need to communicate using pictures, signs, or computers instead of speech.

Physical Therapy Services   A physical therapist helps a child develop and use motor skills related to coordination, balance, muscle strength, endurance, range of motion, and mobility. The physical therapist develops specific exercises to help a child learn to move the large muscles of his or her body for activities such as crawling,

Name: William Student   **School:** Martin Luther King, Jr. E.S.

Annual Goals and Short-Term Objectives

Area of Instruction: Language
Goal 1

William will indicate the area of the room he wishes to use during choice time.

Objective 1: Review Date 1/94
William will choose the picture of his desired play area and take it to the area.

Evaluation Criteria:
4/5 opportunities of choice time during a 1-month period

Objective 2: Review Date 6/94
William will name the area of the room where he wants to play during choice time.

Evaluation Criteria:
4/5 opportunities of choice time during a 1-month period

Area of Instruction: Cognition

Goal 2

William will identify objects by their shape.

Objective 1: Review Date 1/94
William will match objects by their shape (e.g., when he puts the blocks away in the block corner).

Evaluation Criteria:
4/5 opportunities during a 1-month period

Objective 2: Review Date 6/94
William will identify objects by name (e.g., square, rectangle, triangle, circle).

Evaluation Criteria:
4/5 opportunities during a 1-month period

Figure 5.   Page 3 of a sample IEP.

walking, running, jumping, and climbing. The therapist also may make specific suggestions for special equipment, such as braces, wheelchairs, or walkers to help a child learn to move as independently as possible.

Occupational Therapy Services   The occupational therapist specializes in fine motor, oral motor, perceptual-motor, sensory processing, and activities of daily living. The therapist may use activities to help the child organize incoming information from all the senses (visual, tactile, auditory, balance) that he or she receives. Sensory information combined appropriately with movement results in better quality skills for many play, learning, and self-help activities. The occupational therapist helps children learn to use writing implements and playground equipment, and complete puzzles and participate in art activities. Activities of daily living such as learning to eat, dress, and use the bathroom independently also might be part of a child's occupational therapy program.

Integrated Services

One of the most effective ways to provide services to children with disabilities is to make them part of the regular classroom routine. As much as possible, therapeutic activities should have a clear purpose for the child during his or her daily routine. For example, dressing skills should be practiced when coats are put on and taken off before and after going outside. This promotes learning in a natural context. This type of service delivery needs careful coordination among all staff (i.e., sufficient time for goal setting, planning and completing activities) and ongoing communication to monitor progress. The following example describes a situation that staff often encounter when beginning to include children in new settings.

◄◦► ◄◦► ◄◦►

Including children with disabilities in the regular classroom was a new idea at Madison Children's Center. Ms. Stevens, the classroom teacher, and Ms. Dobbins, the speech-language therapist, found that they needed to talk on a regular basis to plan and coordinate activities. No planning time had been set aside in the schedule, so temporarily they met during their lunch hour once every 2 weeks to develop their activities together. They had an appointment with the center's director to discuss how the schedule could be rearranged to give them a regular planning time in their schedules.

There were three children in the room eligible for speech-language services. After looking at the children's IEPs, Ms. Stevens and Ms. Dobbins determined the skills that needed to be targeted for the next 2 weeks. They decided the theme would be Community Helpers and planned activities that would fit the theme and include the use of the targeted skills. For example, Freddy needed to increase his vocabulary about food items so they planned to set up a small grocery store where the children could pretend to be sales clerks and customers buying food. Ms. Dobbins also planned to go on the field trip to the grocery store and spend time with Freddy looking at and naming food items.

◄◦► ◄◦► ◄◦►

DIFFICULTIES IN OBTAINING SPECIAL EDUCATION SERVICES

There are many steps in applying for and obtaining special education services. The family and child need your support as they make their way through this maze. It is frustrating for everyone when the school system process seems to move slowly, so it helps if parents and teachers understand how the school system works and how to be good advocates by persisting in seeking the services their children need.

The concepts of mainstreaming, integration, and inclusion remain controversial in some communities. Because public school systems rarely provide programs for typical children, ages 3 to 5, there often are no natural opportunities for the children in special education programs to interact with children without disabilities. As movement for inclusion gains momentum, more school systems are considering new options, such as providing some special education services in community settings like part-time preschool programs and full-time child care programs. Slowly, changes in services are providing more opportunities for integrated education. Parents also are beginning to ask school systems to support a continuum of inclusion opportunities for their children with disabilities, by providing special education services in regular early childhood programs. Successful inclusive services for all children depend on cooperation, coordination, and collaboration between public schools and private community programs.

Bringing Inclusion into the Classroom
Teaching Issues

Specific staff concerns related to including children with disabilities are addressed in this part. Information is provided about specific disabilities, guidelines for communicating with families, and classroom adaptations for children with special needs. Chapter 12, written by Janeen McCrakcn Taylor, provides information about including children with special health care needs and guidelines for keeping all children in group settings healthy.

8
Parent–Teacher Communication

A comfortable relationship between teacher and parent makes it easier for everyone to work together to help the child. Good communication is the key to that relationship.

Often this relationship develops without much effort, but sometimes relationships get off on the wrong foot as one person's efforts at communication are misunderstood by the other person. Parents may hear only criticism; teachers may feel parents are uncooperative. Communication is a two-way street and both teachers and parents can feel frustrated when well-intentioned comments are given unintended meanings. Teachers and parents rely on each other for information about how children feel and act both at home and in child care. Open communication can make them strong allies as they work together to nurture and support the children they love.

When a child has a disability, a good relationship between the parent and the teacher is especially important. The teacher and the parents need to be able to talk openly about difficult and emotionally painful topics. For parents, talking about their child's disability can remind them of their child's limitations and make them fearful that their child will be treated differently or will be asked to leave the program.

The following comments from teachers and parents reveal the concerns they feel when a child with a disability begins a new program, *"I decided not to tell the preschool that Matthew had cerebral palsy. I didn't want them to treat him any differently. I just wanted him to be one of the kids."*

One mother said, *"I worried every day that the teacher would tell me that Jacob was too much trouble and he would have to leave the program. It was such a relief to learn that other children had bad days too."*

Teachers also may be reluctant to raise potentially difficult topics. They may be afraid that they will upset the parents or they may feel that they do not know enough about the child and the disability. Teachers may decide that discussions related to the disability are better left to other professionals who specialize in that area.

One teacher remembered, *"I wanted to know if I could expect Marjorie to follow the same rules as the other children. I didn't know if I should expect her to help put the toys away at clean-up time. But I didn't want to ask her mother because I was afraid she would think that Marjorie was misbehaving."*

Another teacher commented, *"I noticed that Malcolm wasn't eating snacks and he seemed unusually quiet. I wondered if his behavior might mean that something was wrong with his shunt, but I hesitated to mention it to his mother because I didn't feel it was my place to discuss medical matters."*

Sean did well at the Children's Center but his teacher, Ms. Harnes, immediately noticed that Sean walked slowly and awkwardly, had trouble going up and down stairs, and fell frequently on the playground. His gross motor skills were far behind those of the other children in the class. His teacher explained:

◄o► ◄o► ◄o►

I wondered if I should talk with Sean's parents. I'm sure they had noticed his problems. Was there something I should be doing to help Sean? Was it safe to let him try climbing and running?

◄o► ◄o► ◄o►

After speaking with her director, Ms. Harnes scheduled a meeting with Sean's parents. At the meeting, when she talked about her concerns, Sean's parents explained about the cerebral palsy and mentioned their reluctance to talk about it earlier for fear that Sean would be treated differently. They let her know that Sean could participate in all activities even though he might fall more frequently.

◄o► ◄o► ◄o►

After the meeting, I was relieved but I was also upset. Why didn't Sean's parents tell me about his problems right away? Didn't they realize that I needed this information to help Sean succeed in the classroom? I decided that in the future, I would ask parents directly to please tell me if their child has any special needs I should know about so I can help them succeed in the classroom. I also will make it a point to tell each parent that all children are welcome in my classroom.

◄o► ◄o► ◄o►

When teachers and parents are reluctant to talk about difficult topics, they need to remember that the child's interests are best served by an honest and open sharing of information.

GROUND RULES

Relationships do not happen overnight. They take time and attention to develop and flourish. Here are some guidelines to keep in mind whenever you talk to parents.

Create an Atmosphere of Trust and Understanding

Encourage a positive exchange of information. Ask parents what they want to know about their child's day. Let them know that you are on their side and want to work with them to provide the best experience for their child. Consider scheduling a conference shortly after the child enrolls to talk with the family about their expectations, goals, and concerns. This meeting can be a wonderful opportunity to get to know each other before any problem arises.

One parent commented, *"I was surprised when Johnny's teacher asked to meet with us. He had been at the center for just 2 weeks. She told us how he was adjusting and she asked us what we hoped he would learn in her class. I really appreciated her interest. After that meeting I knew she would take good care of Johnny and I felt like I could talk to her whenever I had a question."*

Communicate in a Variety of Ways

Notes, newsletters, informal conversations in the hall, and telephone calls help you stay in frequent contact. This regular communication strengthens the developing relationship and helps parents and teachers gradually get to know each other better. It also helps parents feel that they are free to talk to you about their concerns outside of a formal conference time. One parent appreciated written information about her son, *"The weekly newsletter was so important to me. It was the only way I knew what activities were going to happen each day. It helped me know what to ask Jamal about when he came home."*

Another parent said, *"I loved the notes that Margaret brought home from school. They were just a line or two but they let me know how her day went and they reassured me that she was having fun even though she couldn't tell me in so many words."*

Take Time to Communicate with the Family

Think about communication from the parents' perspective. Imagine that you are the parent of a child with a disability. Your child comes home from school and she cannot tell you about her day. You worry about whether she ate her lunch, whether another child hit her, or just if she had a good time. As you think about communication from the parents' point of view you can better understand why many parents are hungry for as much information about their child as you can give them. When a child has difficulty communicating, the parent really has no idea what goes on each day unless you tell him or her. Mom and Dad cannot talk about school with their child unless they know about some of the major events. It also will be easier to raise a difficult subject if you communicate regularly with the family. Give short progress reports frequently to let the parents know how things are going. Sean's father reported:

◄o► ◄o► ◄o►

Before Sean attended the Children's Center, he went to a special education program. Every day the teacher sent home a summary of what the class did. It told about the art activity and circle time, and included comments that the children had made. Sean had a notebook that went with him everywhere. His special education teacher wrote in it as did his physical and occupational therapists. His mother and I also wrote in it. This way everyone working with Sean stayed in close touch.

When Sean went to the Children's Center, we missed this regular contact. We were used to knowing everything that happened during Sean's day. He was old enough now to tell us about parts of his day, but like any child he was not as forthcoming about the details as we would have liked.

I called Ms. Harnes and told her about the notebook Sean had in his other school. I asked if she would be willing to try it. Ms. Harnes was very enthusiastic. She had been wanting to know more about Sean, and this way she and Sean's physical therapist would be able to communicate with us and with each other through the notebook. She told me that she thought it was a great idea and that she would try to write something at least every other day.

The notebook system worked well for everyone. My wife and I were less worried now that we knew more about Sean's day. His physical therapist learned about the problems he was having on the playground and was able to make some suggestions. At school, Ms. Harnes was able to use those suggestions and ask for other ideas to help Sean manage the stairs.

◄o► ◄o► ◄o►

Focus on Strengths

Parents often are used to hearing about what is wrong with their child. You need to build a relationship on the strengths of the family and the child, not on the weaknesses. Let parents know about the small successes you see on a daily basis. Tell them about the ways their child is like his or her typical peers.

Jenny's mother reported, *"About 2 weeks after Jenny started school, her teacher called to tell me that she had used the slide for the first time that day. I can't tell you how much that short phone call meant to me. The teacher really seemed to know Jenny and to like her. After that I started to relax and think that maybe Jenny did belong with regular kids after all."*

Trust Yourself

As the teacher, you see the child daily and come to know intimately his or her likes, dislikes, routines, and unique characteristics. Do not underestimate how much you really do know about the child, and do not let the disability frighten you into thinking that you know less about this child than you do about the other children in your class.

Parents do not expect you to be an expert in special education. In most situations there will be several people who provide specialized services to the child that directly address the disability. Parents want you to see to it that their child is safe, happy, and a valued member of the group. Your unique contribution is your knowledge of the child in the context of other children without disabilities. Your perspective allows you to see all the ways the child with a disability is similar to the "regular kids." Sean's teacher, Ms. Harnes, commented:

◄○► ◄○► ◄○►

In a few weeks, I got to know Sean well. I learned that he loved art activities and books, he was an eager contributor at circle time, and he was very polite. He also talked more to adults than to children and frequently needed reassurances from me. He rarely approached other children and most often played by himself.

I also learned from Sean that he had physical therapy several times a week. Sean would often announce, "My physical therapist says I can do this by myself."

Over time, I became less concerned about Sean's cerebral palsy. I knew he was getting the services he needed and I worried more about helping him make friends in the classroom.

I decided to have another short meeting with Sean's parents. I let them know that Sean was doing well. They had a lot of questions and wanted to know if the other children teased Sean and if Sean's language and social skills seemed appropriate for his age.

I was able to reassure them and let them know that Sean was happy and that I was encouraging him to play with the other children.

◄○► ◄○► ◄○►

Understanding your role and what parents expect of you can make it easier to establish open avenues of communication.

Respect the Individuality of Each Family

Each family comes with its own set of values and beliefs. If you can meet with the family shortly after their child enters the center you can talk with them about their expectations. It is important to appreciate and respect their values, goals, and concerns even when they are different from your own. Start with the assumption that parents want what is best for their child. They have the lifelong responsibility of caring for their child and they have the right to make final decisions in all matters. Carrie's mother recalls a meeting with Carrie's teacher about speech-language therapy.

◄○► ◄○► ◄○►

Carrie had just been tested by the public schools and they recommended that she start speech-language therapy as soon as possible. We were reluctant. We met with the teacher and talked about our concerns for overburdening Carrie. Carrie didn't like to be rushed and she already was tired at the end of the day. We felt strongly that such a young child should not be over scheduled.

Carrie's teacher understood our concerns, but he also was worried about how delayed Carrie's speech was. He told us that he felt speech-language therapy would really help Carrie learn to talk and that she should start as soon as possible.

After thinking about it carefully, we decided to wait 2 months until the summer when I could arrange my work schedule so I could pick Carrie up early once a week and take her to speech-language therapy. The program at school was less structured in the summer so we felt Carrie would not feel so hurried. Carrie's teacher was disappointed but he understood our reasoning.

◄o► ◄o► ◄o►

Keep Information Confidential

Sometimes parents of other children will ask you about the child with a disability. They may want to know how the child's presence is affecting the rest of the class, they might have specific questions about the disability, or they might want some information to help them talk with their own child about differences and disabilities. When this happens, give them the information they need without violating the privacy of the child with a disability and his or her family. Try to prepare for this possibility before it arises by asking the parents of a child with a disability how they would like you to handle questions. Ms. Harnes wanted more information about Sean.

◄o► ◄o► ◄o►

When the Johnsons told me that Sean had cerebral palsy, I asked them for some information so I could learn more about the condition. I also asked how they would like me to handle any questions other children or adults might ask.

The Johnsons did not want me to use the words "cerebral palsy" but requested that I tell people that the muscles in Sean's legs didn't work right, that he was born this way, and that he was learning special exercises to help him.

I was comfortable with this and promised to let the Johnsons know if other questions arose.

◄o► ◄o► ◄o►

Ms. Harnes now has permission from the Johnsons to talk about the differences in Sean that others might notice. She can explain to the other children why Sean does not run fast and she can respond to questions that other parents might have. If necessary, she can return to the Johnsons and talk with them about how to handle other issues that might arise. For example, if Sean used any special equipment, such as braces or a walker, his mother might come to school to talk with the other children and give them an opportunity to use the equipment.

When other people ask questions about a child's disability, it is important to respect the child's privacy. By talking with parents about the issue before it arises, you can be prepared to respond in a manner consistent with the family's wishes.

WHAT PARENTS WANT

As you begin to build positive relationships with families, it helps to understand their perspective. What parents want from you is a recognition of their efforts and an appreciation of their concern and love for their child.

Time

Most of all, parents want someone who will take the time to listen to them. Let them know that you will make time for them. Consider scheduling a regular time that parents can reach you by telephone. For example, you could let families know that they can reach you on Tuesdays between 1 P.M. and 2 P.M. You also could set aside one afternoon a week for parents to talk with you briefly and post a sign-up sheet outside your room. Sometimes it may be easier for you to call the family. In this case, parents can request a telephone call and you can return calls at a set time, for example, on Wednesday between 8:30 P.M. and 9 P.M.

Information

Parents need clear, accurate, and complete information on the center, your classroom, and their child's activities. One teacher related:

Tameka's mother wanted to know if the farm we were planning to visit on a field trip would have bathrooms available for the children. She was working very hard with Tameka on toilet training and she didn't want Tameka to have an accident and be embarrassed if no facilities were available. I called the farm and explained the situation. They told me that Tameka could use the restroom in the office if she needed to. I told Tameka's mother and she thanked me for putting her fears to rest.

Parents do not expect you to know everything. When you do not know, admit it. Parents do expect you to talk with them honestly and openly. They want straight answers, not jargon or evasion. One mother explained:

I asked Caleb's teacher for some ideas for toilet training him. She said that she didn't really know anything specific for children with Down syndrome but that she would see what she could find out. A few days later she gave me the telephone number of a behavior

specialist and a brochure on toilet training. It made me realize that she really does care about Caleb and that she is on my side.

◄o► ◄o► ◄o►

Care and Compassion

Parents may have had experiences in which their child was not accepted, and they may have received a lot of bad news from professionals. You can help by recognizing their concerns. Your willingness to talk openly communicates that you care about their feelings and that you too want what is best for their child. Katherine's father appreciated her teacher's input about her "new" vocabulary:

◄o► ◄o► ◄o►

I still remember the doctor telling us that Katherine would never walk or talk. She was just a baby and I felt like her life was over. Now I look at her with her friends and I can't believe how far we've all come. Her teacher told me last week that Katherine was using "bathroom words" during snack time and that we need to work on this. This was my child who was never going to talk and now she's saying "bad" words.

◄o► ◄o► ◄o►

Miguel's mother remembers:

◄o► ◄o► ◄o►

I was so nervous about Miguel being in a "regular" classroom. Every day I was afraid his teacher would tell me that he had done something wrong and that he didn't belong. One day she asked to speak to me and told me there was a problem in the class. She must have seen the look on my face because she rushed to tell me, "No, no, the problem is not Miguel. He is doing really well. I just wanted to let you know so you could discuss the situation with Miguel if he brings it up."

I was so relieved. Two other children were having a problem playing together with the blocks. My Miguel was not the problem. I realized that other children weren't perfect either and that Miguel's teacher really thought he belonged.

◄o► ◄o► ◄o►

WHAT TEACHERS NEED

Teachers want and need many of the same things as parents. Let parents know how they can help you. Here are some things you might talk about.

Information

You need to know things about the child and family that might affect the child at school. If parents understand why you need this information, they will be more willing to discuss things with you. Lottie's teacher needed to understand Lottie's unusual behavior:

◄○► ◄○► ◄○►

Lottie had suddenly started spending a lot of time in the doll corner. She wrapped the dolls in blankets, held them close, and gave them bottles. When I tried to entice Lottie to join the class at group time, Lottie cried and protested. I was puzzled because Lottie had never been interested in the dolls before.

On Friday, I asked Lottie's mother if anything was different at home. I explained about Lottie's new interest in dolls. Lottie's mother smiled and said that her sister had visited over the weekend and brought her new baby. This was the first time that Lottie had been around an infant and she was fascinated.

Monday morning I talked with Lottie about her new cousin. Lottie showed me how she had rocked the baby. Gradually, Lottie began to play with other toys again and was able to leave her dolls to join the class during group time.

◄○► ◄○► ◄○►

Trust

When you ask about the child's disability, you want the family to trust that you will not misuse the information or treat the child inappropriately. Let the family know that you will use the information for the good of the child.

Feedback

Everyone needs to be appreciated. Parents should acknowledge your skills and professionalism. Let them know you take pride in your job.

Communication works both ways. You let parents know what happens in school and you need to know what happens at home. How does the child feel about coming to school? How do the parents feel about what you are doing in the classroom? Patrick's teacher related her experience:

◄○► ◄○► ◄○►

After the visit to the pumpkin patch, Patrick's mother called me.

"Patrick is having a hard time with Halloween this year. He's afraid of witches and ghosts. We have to look under his bed with a flashlight before he'll go to sleep. He saw a scarecrow at the pumpkin patch and now he's afraid there will be a witch in the classroom."

I thanked her for the telephone call. When Patrick arrived at school I met him at the door and told him that no witches or ghosts were allowed in our room. At group time I talked about how Halloween could be scary sometimes. Several children said that they were afraid that monsters would get them.

I also decided to send a letter home to all the parents alerting them to possible negative reactions to Halloween and giving them ideas to help them reassure their children.

PLANNING A PARENT CONFERENCE

When it is time for a formal conference with a child's parents, think through the process in advance. Find out what parents want to meet about and what questions they have, and then gather the information you will need. This might include reports on the child, information from other professionals, or community resources with names and telephone numbers.

Next, develop a plan and rehearse the meeting in your mind.

- Who will be at the conference?
- What do you want to tell the parents?
- What will you say first?
- How do you think they will react?
- How would you feel if you were the parent in this situation?
- What do you want the outcome of the conference to be?

Finally, schedule a convenient time and find a quiet, private space to meet. To schedule the conference try to talk with parents in person or call them on the telephone. Tell them the purpose of the meeting, and, in families with two parents, encourage both parents to attend. Let everyone know how long the conference will last.

Guidelines for Parent–Teacher Conferences

1. Start the conference on a positive note. Tell a short anecdote about something good the child has done in the classroom.
2. Avoid jargon. State the reason for wanting to talk with the parents in plain language.
3. Give examples of what you see in the classroom. Be specific and do not make assumptions or jump to conclusions.
4. Invite the parents to tell you how they see their child.
5. If there is a problem, work with the parents to develop a plan of action to address the problem. Try to have referral numbers and books or other resources available.
6. Remember that the parents may be as nervous as you are.
7. Give information, not advice.
8. Take notes and write down the main points that were discussed so you can refer to them later.
9. Summarize at the end of the meeting and decide with the parents on the next steps.

Even if you follow these guidelines, there will be times when the conference does not go well and parents become upset or angry. Sean's teacher describes her experience:

◄o► ◄o► ◄o►

In the spring, I asked to meet with Sean's parents. I knew they were trying to decide whether or not to send Sean to kindergarten in the fall and I wanted to talk with them about Sean's progress during the year. They were anxious about making this decision and I wanted to allow enough time to discuss the issue thoroughly.

I arranged to use the director's office and told the Johnsons we would be able to meet for an hour. Then I collected some of Sean's work from his file, including paintings, drawings, and some dictated stories. I went over my anecdotal records and behavioral observations so I would be able to give the Johnsons some specific examples of what Sean had learned in the last few months.

I started the conference by telling Sean's parents how much progress he had made. I reminded them that at the beginning of the year Sean had looked for a lot of adult attention and had rarely played with other children. Now, he was quite independent and had two good friends in the class. The other children liked him, and he played comfortably in small groups. His language skills were excellent and he dictated complex stories. He still had difficulty using a crayon, and his drawings were not as detailed as some of the other children's. I ended by saying that I believed Sean was ready for kindergarten.

The Johnsons were upset to hear that Sean's drawing skills were not on a par with those of the other children. How would he be able to write his letters in kindergarten? He was small for his age and, coupled with his cerebral palsy, wouldn't it be better to wait another year?

I gently reminded the Johnsons that Sean's birthday was in February so he would already be 5½ when he started kindergarten. Besides, his two best friends would be going to the same school. I suggested that they visit the kindergarten class and talk with the teacher. I told them that I felt Sean had both the skills and the maturity to do well in kindergarten. He might need extra help with hand-writing, but that was related to his cerebral palsy and it might not improve much even in another year.

We talked for the full hour. Even then they had not reached any decision, but they understood the reasons for my recommendation and promised to talk about it.

◄o► ◄o► ◄o►

If Ms. Harnes had recommended that Sean remain in preschool for another year, the Johnsons might have been quite upset even though they were considering the same possibility. They could have interpreted that recommendation to mean that Sean was not doing well in school and that his cerebral palsy was a big problem. Ms. Harnes might have become defensive and given lots of specific examples of how Sean was different from the other children. The conference could have ended with the Johnsons feeling hurt and worried about Sean and Ms. Harnes upset that her intentions were misunderstood.

Talking with parents on a regular basis will make it easier to bring up difficult subjects. Remember that parents want to know that you care about their child. They want you to be sensitive as well as honest. Regular communication will help you do a better job in the classroom and it will help the parents do a better job at home. When teachers and parents work together, the child has a better chance for a good school experience.

Learning About Disabilities

A child with a disability is a child first, and shares the same feelings, needs, and interests as typical children. This child also has some needs that are different from those of typical children. Remember that the disability is only one piece of information about the child. Knowing the name of the disability tells you very little about how the child learns or how best to teach him or her. It does not tell you what his or her later abilities might be. Applying a diagnostic label may be necessary to determine a child's eligibility for services, but learning about who the child is and what he or she needs must go beyond that label or diagnosis.

DEFINITIONS ACCORDING TO IDEA

In an earlier chapter you learned the definition of a *qualified individual with a disability* from the Americans with Disabilities Act (ADA). Most of the children with disabilities who qualify under the Individuals with Disabilities Education Act (IDEA) also would be considered to have a disability under the ADA.

The following descriptions are the most common disability categories defined by IDEA. A disability must adversely affect educational performance for a child to receive special education services under IDEA. Chapter 3 describes this law in more detail and Chapter 5 provides specific information about how to adjust your teaching strategies and learning activities to accommodate a variety of learners. The Resources section at the end of this book lists where to find additional information about specific disabilities.

Remember that children's diagnoses will vary and their learning needs must be considered individually. As you read these descriptions, think about how you would teach such a child.

Autism

Autism is a developmental disability that significantly affects verbal and nonverbal communication and social interaction. It is generally evident before age 3. Other characteristics often associated with autism are engagement in repetitive activities and stereotyped movements, resistance to environmental change or change in daily routines, and unusual responses to sensory experiences.

◄o► ◄o► ◄o►

Peter is 3 years old and has been attending preschool since he was 18 months old. The first thing his teacher noticed was that he preferred to play alone and took very little notice of the other children. When she held him, he tended to pull away. When he was upset, he was difficult to comfort, and holding him didn't help.

Now, at age 3 Peter doesn't talk spontaneously and often repeats what is said to him. He gets upset and cries if the routine of the day is changed or if one of the classroom staff is absent. He likes to line up all of his toys and will not allow anyone to move them. Peter is good at putting puzzles together and loves to look at books. He always notices the new library books and goes through each one of them. He has just started to name some toys in the classroom.

◄o► ◄o► ◄o►

Robert avoids looking directly at people and spends a lot of time walking around the periphery of the room. He has particular toys that he likes and becomes angry when asked to share them with other children. Although he is 3, the teacher has never heard him say a word except for reciting television commercials. One day during an art activity she was amazed to see Robert writing letters with his marker. His teacher asked his mother if that was something she was working on at home. His mother said, "No, but Robert watches "Sesame Street" frequently." He also refuses to eat lunch at school. His mother reports that he is a very "picky" eater at home and she fixes only his favorite foods.

◄o► ◄o► ◄o►

Deafness

Deafness is a hearing impairment that is so severe that a child is unable to hear and understand spoken words, with or without amplification.

◄o► ◄o► ◄o►

Samantha was born quite prematurely and only weighed 3¾ pounds. She spent a lot of time in the "preemie nursery" before she could go home. Although she was very tiny, she developed well and her parents were pleased until they noticed that she didn't seem to turn toward the sound of their voices or notice when the dog was barking. The pediatrician sent the family to an audiologist who diagnosed a severe hearing loss. The audiologist recommended a program for children who have hearing impairments. A teacher began coming to the house to teach Samantha and her parents sign language.

Deaf-Blindness

Deaf-blindness means concomitant hearing and visual impairments, the combination of which causes such significant communication and other developmental and educational problems that children cannot be accommodated in special education programs solely for children with blindness.

Tia's mother had a slight infection while she was pregnant, but she did not notice anything unusual about her pregnancy. When Tia was born, the doctor immediately noticed that she had difficulty breathing and that she was stiff and irritable. She nursed poorly and lost a lot of weight. After a thorough examination, it was determined that Tia was both deaf and blind and had delayed motor development. The infection that Tia's mother had is called cytomegalovirus, which causes severe damage to the development of a fetus if contracted in the first trimester of pregnancy.

Hearing Impairment

Hearing impairment means that an individual has a hearing loss, whether permanent or fluctuating.

Jason wore a hearing aid to school. The other children asked about it and Jason's mother came to class to talk about Jason's hearing aids and let the other children try them on. She reminded the children that it was important for Jason to see the face and mouth of the person talking to him because sometimes he could "see" what he or she was saying. She also said that sometimes they would have to show him how to do things rather than explain it to him. She said that Jason sounded funny when he talked because he couldn't hear what he said very well.

◄◦► ◄◦► ◄◦►

Mental Retardation

Mental retardation is significantly below-average general intellectual functioning existing concurrently with limitations in adaptive behavior. Adaptive behavior refers to the ability to meet the demands of the environment through age-appropriate, independent skills in self-care, communication, and play.

◄○► ◄○► ◄○►

Melissa was born with Down syndrome. The doctor was very helpful and supportive when explaining the condition to her parents. Both of Melissa's parents were very upset, but they began to read books about Down syndrome. They visited an early intervention program for infants with disabilities and talked to other parents of children with Down syndrome. One thing that they learned was that children with Down syndrome almost always have some degree of mental retardation. Melissa's parents weren't sure what this meant or what to expect. At the age of 6 months, Melissa started in the early intervention program and they realized that her development was like that of her older brother, but much slower. She walked much later and didn't begin to talk until she was 3. Learning new things took Melissa a long time and she needed lots of practice until she was able to perform skills independently.

◄○► ◄○► ◄○►

The next time Ms. James went to see her son's pediatrician, she requested a developmental evaluation for her son Corey even though the pediatrician assured her that he was developing well during the last visit. Ms. James was very worried about Corey. Although he was a very happy baby, he seemed too quiet. She remembered that Corey's brother Jonathon was a lot more active at this age. By the age of 18 months Jonathon was walking well by himself, could use his hands well to hold and play with toys, and said a few words. Corey wasn't walking or manipulating toys well.

The psychologist confirmed Ms. James' suspicion that Corey's development was delayed. Together they reviewed her pregnancy and Corey's birth history, but no causes for the delay in development were apparent. The psychologist suggested that Ms. James contact the local early intervention program where there were teachers and therapists who could give her suggestions for ways to work with Corey and stimulate his development.

◄○► ◄○► ◄○►

Multiple Disabilities

Multiple disabilities means concomitant impairments (e.g., mental retardation and blindness, mental retardation and an orthopedic impairment), the combination of which causes such significant educational problems that children cannot be accommodated in a program solely for one of the impairments.

Ms. Freeman had a very difficult delivery and her baby Latavia did not get enough oxygen. The lack of oxygen caused brain injury that resulted in cerebral palsy and cortical blindness. The doctor said that Latavia would always need someone to care for her. She now attends a special education program where she also receives occupational, physical, and speech-language therapy.

Orthopedic Impairment

Orthopedic impairment is any condition that involves muscles, bones, or joints and is characterized by difficulty with movement. The term includes impairments caused by congenital anomaly (e.g., clubfoot, absence of a body limb), impairments caused by disease (e.g., poliomyelitis, bone tuberculosis), and impairments from other causes (e.g., cerebral palsy, amputations, and fractures or burns that cause contractures). In educational or noneducational settings it affects the ability to perform small or large muscle activities or to perform self-help skills.

Felicia has trouble keeping up with her classmates on the playground. She runs with a slight stiffness in her left leg, and her left arm is held tightly against her body. She is not quite as adventurous as her friends because she loses her balance and trips often. Her mother explained to the teacher that Felicia was born prematurely with brain injury that left her with a slight paralysis on the left side. Felicia leaves school early twice a week and proudly tells her friends she is going to visit her "PT" to do her exercises.

John is a very sociable child who loves to talk with his friends and teachers. He was born with an opening in his spinal cord that had to be surgically closed. This condition is called spina bifida. *The nerves were damaged below the opening in his spine and he does not have any feelings in his legs and can't move them. Shortly after birth he also had increased pressure in his brain and the doctor inserted a device called a* shunt *to help drain the extra spinal fluid and relieve the pressure. John wears braces on his legs to support his weight when he walks with crutches. He recently got a motorized wheelchair for school because walking is so difficult.*

Other Health Impairments

Other health impairments include conditions that limit strength, vitality, or alertness due to a chronic or acute health problem. Examples of chronic or acute health problems include cancer, some neurological disorders, rheumatic fever, severe asthma, uncontrolled seizure disorders, heart conditions, lead poisoning, diabetes, acquired immunodeficiency syndrome (AIDS), blood disorders (e.g., hemophilia, sickle cell anemia), cystic fibrosis, heart disease, and attention deficit disorder.

◄o► ◄o► ◄o►

When Amelia came to school her teacher did not notice that she had a disability. Amelia's mother wrote a note explaining that her daughter has a congenital heart defect. She also sent a note from Amelia's doctor assuring the school that it was okay for Amelia to attend school with her friends. The doctor's note went on to say that Amelia could participate in all activities, but if she seemed out of breath or became a little blue around her mouth or on her finger-nails, she should sit quietly until her color returned to normal. Amelia loved school and did everything the other children did. Her friends joined her whenever she needed a "quiet play time."

◄o► ◄o► ◄o►

Jarron is a very active 3-year-old who loves to run, climb, and chase. His favorite time of day is "Outside Time." When Jarron was 2½ years old, his parents began to notice that he would get out of breath easily. They also noticed that he had trouble breathing when he got too excited or when the pollen count was high. As he got a little older, this shortness of breath continued and he began to have audible wheezing. The doctor diagnosed Jarron as having asthma and for a short time he had to have regular treatments on a special machine. His mother talked to the school director so that he would know what to do if Jarron started to have trouble breathing at school.

◄o► ◄o► ◄o►

Severe Emotional Disturbance

Severe emotional disturbance describes behavioral or emotional responses that a child experiences that are extremely different from other children with the same ethnic or cultural background. These extreme behaviors impair social relationships and adaptive skills and are very disruptive in the classroom.

1. Severe emotional disturbance refers to a condition that results one or more of the following characteristics over a long period of time, and to a marked degree, that adversely affects a child's educational performance:

   a. An inability to learn that cannot be explained by intellec-tual, sensory, or health factors

   b. An inability to build or maintain satisfactory interpersonal relationships with peers and teachers

   c. Inappropriate types of behavior or feelings under normal circumstances

   d. A general pervasive mood of unhappiness or depression

   e. A tendency to develop physical symptoms or fears associated with personal or school problems

2. Severe emotional disturbance includes schizophrenia. The term does not apply to children who are socially maladjusted, unless it is determined that they have a serious emotional disturbance.

It is unusual for young children to be given this diagnosis. Usually, extreme behaviors in young children are related to autism, mental retardation, acquired brain injury, or general developmental delay. Sometimes these behaviors result from early trauma such as abuse or neglect.

Specific Learning Disability

Specific learning disability is a disorder in one or more of the basic *psychological* processes involved in understanding or using spoken or written language. Children may have difficulty listening, thinking, speaking, writing, spelling, and doing mathematical calculations. The term includes such conditions as perceptual disabilities, acquired brain injury, minimal brain dysfunction, dyslexia, and developmental aphasia. The term does not apply to children who have learning problems that are primarily the result of visual or hearing impairments; motor disabilities; mental retardation; emotional disturbance; or environmental, cultural, or economic disadvantage. Although this definition usually does not apply to preschool-age children, teachers may notice children who have trouble acquiring the *beginning* skills for reading, writing, spelling, or doing math.

◄○► ◄○► ◄○►

Fred's mother remembers that in preschool his teacher told her that Fred was "all boy" and had no interest in any table or art activities. He preferred physical activities and pretend games like Ninja Turtles. When he participated in "sharing time," he seemed to have a lot of general knowledge and a very good memory.

   Now Fred was in first grade, and handwriting was so frustrating that Fred hated to write anything. Although he could repeat whole stories that were read to him, he couldn't seem to make sense of letters and words. Fred's teacher told his mother that he just didn't seem motivated. His mother didn't understand how Fred could easily do his math problems and put together complicated models, but be unable to recognize simple words. One day the reading teacher called and said she suspected that Fred might have a learning disability. The subsequent testing proved her right. With the help of a resource teacher who works with Fred on visual perception and fine motor skills, all of Fred's schoolwork has started to improve and he seems much happier.

◄o► ◄o► ◄o►

This category is very broad and it may be difficult to distinguish a learning disability from other learning problems, especially in a young child. Each school system develops its own criteria for determining if a child has a learning disability. Contact your local special education department in the public school for its definition.

Speech or Language Impairments

Speech or language impairments are communication disorders such as stuttering, impaired articulation, or voice impairment. This category also includes the inability to express oneself or an inability to understand what is being said.

◄o► ◄o► ◄o►

The teacher had a great deal of difficulty understanding what Lydia was saying. She knew that young children often mispronounced some words, but Lydia's trouble seemed more severe. In the classroom she understood everything that was said to her and followed directions well. Much of the time the teacher had to have Lydia show her what she wanted because she couldn't figure out what Lydia was trying to say.

◄o► ◄o► ◄o►

Alan had a very good vocabulary and had wonderful conversations with his teacher. However, when the teacher asked Alan a question, he would often get a perplexed look on his face and just repeat the question. The teacher knew that Alan knew the answer because they had talked about it before. She was very puzzled and didn't know what to think of Alan's inability to answer questions.

◄o► ◄o► ◄o►

Traumatic Brain Injury

Traumatic brain injury[1] is an injury to the brain caused by an external physical force, resulting in total or partial functional disability or psychosocial impairment, or both. The term applies to open or closed head injuries resulting in impairments in one or more areas, such as cognition; language; memory; attention; reasoning; abstract thinking; judgment; problem solving; sensory, perceptual, and motor abilities; psychosocial behavior; physical functions; information processing; and speech. The term does not apply to brain injuries that are congenital or degenerative or brain injuries induced by birth trauma.

---

[1]Although the preferred terminology for this disability has been changed to *acquired brain injury*, traumatic brain injury is used here because it is the term used in IDEA.

◄○► ◄○► ◄○►

When Jeffrey was 2 years old he discovered an interesting toy in his father's closet. Unfortunately the "toy" was a gun. The gun went off, hitting Jeffrey in the head. Jeffrey quickly recovered and soon afterward he started preschool. His teacher noticed that the left side of his body didn't work as well as his right side. He seemed to be learning well and could talk clearly, but he had trouble remembering and using the right words. Most of the time he was very friendly and cooperative, but sometimes he had violent tantrums that seemed unprovoked.

◄○► ◄○► ◄○►

Alicia is a happy social child. Her mother was very worried when Alicia had a stroke at 18 months and the doctor said that there might be brain damage. At age 4 Alicia walks with a slight limp and sometimes her right hand gets very stiff. Her language and cognitive skills are well above typical expectations, and Alicia is doing very well in school.

◄○► ◄○► ◄○►

Visual Impairment

Visual impairment is any loss of sight that, with or without correction, adversely affects a child's learning. Blindness refers to a condition with no vision or only light perception. Low vision refers to limited distance vision or the ability to see only items close to the eyes.

◄○► ◄○► ◄○►

When Ahmed was 12 months old his mother noticed that he did not seem to follow moving objects with his eyes. He bumped into things and tripped over toys on the floor. When he looked at books, he held them very close to his face. The next time they visited the pediatrician, Ms. Aziz expressed her concerns. The pediatrician sent them to an ophthalmologist who confirmed that Ahmed had low vision that could not be helped by wearing glasses. He referred them to the vision specialist in the public school system for information and services, who helped Ahmed learn how to explore unfamiliar environments safely and helped Ms. Aziz make their home a safer place to play.

◄○► ◄○► ◄○►

When Sarah was 3 months old, her mother noticed that Sarah did not seem to focus on objects and follow them with her eyes. An examination by the doctor confirmed that Sarah had cataracts. After an operation and the use of contact lenses, Sarah could see much better. She moved around more and became very excited when she saw her parents and the toys that she liked.

◄○► ◄○► ◄○►

DEVELOPMENTAL DELAY

IDEA has an additional category for young children known as *developmental delay*. It is defined as

> Children ages 3 to 5[2] who are experiencing delays, as defined by their state and measured by appropriate diagnostic instruments and procedures, in one or more of the following areas: physical development, cognitive development, communication development, social or emotional development, or adaptive development, and who therefore need education and related services. The extent of the delays may range from mild to severe. (PL 102–119, Sec. 1401 [B] [i])

This category includes

1. Children with identifiable conditions that interfere with their learning and development
2. Children with developmental delays but no apparent biological condition
3. Children who are at risk because of a variety of environmental and biological factors

GUIDELINES FOR TEACHING CHILDREN WITH DIVERSE NEEDS AND LEARNING STYLES

Children need carefully planned environments that provide opportunities to explore and problem-solve actively. Individual, age-appropriate learning opportunities supported by respectful interactions from caregivers allow children to learn at their own rate. A developmentally appropriate program that includes children with disabilities should expect the following:

1. To accept a wide diversity of learning rates and developmental levels of children
2. To modify some activities by breaking them down into several steps and teaching them one piece at a time
3. To adapt materials and activities to meet each child's needs
4. To consult and work with others as part of a team to meet the needs of all the children

Remember that labels do not define children or tell teachers what they need to know about how to teach children. Labels only define disabilities.

---

[2]Some states have chosen to apply this diagnostic category to children younger than 3 years of age or older than 5 years of age.

10

Talking About Disabilities

As you begin to include children with disabilities in your program, the other children and parents will have questions about those differences. Children and adults notice and comment when they see a person who looks or acts different. Differences are what make each person unique. They are not necessarily "good" or "bad," but simply characteristics that make us individuals. One kind of difference is a disability. If you respond to questions about disabilities with clear and accurate information, you let everyone know that it is all right to talk openly about differences. Your words provide a positive model that others can use to talk sensitively and respectfully about differences and disabilities. Your answers help people learn about and understand those differences. Talking about differences, including disabilities, helps all the children and their families. It gives them important information and lets them know that you value and accept each of them.

The adults and children in your program already embody diversity. By acknowledging and accepting variations in age, language, race, size, religion, family composition, and cultural background you help everyone see both similarities and variations. A disability then becomes simply one more difference.

Differences should not overshadow the many things that the children with and without disabilities and their families have in common. As you already know, children with disabilities are children first and are more alike than different from their peers. They share many of the same likes and dislikes as other children, and they need to have friends who care about them and who accept them as valuable members of their community.

PEOPLE-FIRST LANGUAGE

When you talk about anyone who has a disability, it is important to put the person before the special need. A label or diagnosis does not tell you about someone, what he or she is like, what he or she thinks, or what he or she can do. When you put the person first you speak of "children who are deaf" or "the woman who is blind." This puts the emphasis on the person rather than the disability. Using a descriptive term may give more information than a diagnosis— "Jenny has trouble walking," rather than "Jenny has cerebral palsy."

The same rule applies when you talk about any equipment or devices that a person with a disability uses. Refer to a person as using a wheelchair instead of saying "He or she is wheelchair-bound." Talk about a child who wears a hearing aid, rather than an "aided child."

Use the correct name for the disability. For example, Down syndrome is the accepted term, rather than mongoloid. Try to avoid generalizations that tend to glorify the disability, such as "Children with mental retardation are always so happy" or "People with a visual impairment compensate for their loss by developing a better sense of hearing." There is as much variation among people with disabilities as there is within the general population. Describing the disability does not describe the person.

◄o► ◄o► ◄o►

Ms. Stevens told a story about her son Kevin and his friend Greg who lived next door. Kevin and Greg had been best buddies since they were born, but Kevin was bused to a program for children with orthopedic impairments and Greg went to the neighborhood school. At the request of Kevin's parents he was to attend the neighborhood school when appropriate transportation could be arranged. Arrangements were made for a bus with wheelchair tie-downs and transport space. Kevin and Greg were very excited on the first day they were to travel together to the neighborhood school. When Kevin and Greg got on the bus, Greg said, "Kevin, you can't sit there. That's for the kids who are handicapped!" Ms. Stevens said, "I could have hugged Greg. He knows Kevin as his friend and best buddy, not as handicapped."

◄o► ◄o► ◄o►

WHAT CHILDREN NOTICE

Infants and toddlers do notice obvious differences in physical appearance, especially faces that are different. For example, some babies will cry if a stranger approaches, such as a man with a beard who looks different from their clean-shaven father. Babies like to watch other children, but they do not seem disturbed by physical differences in less familiar people.

Children who are 2 and 3 years old notice physical differences but do not always have the verbal ability to ask questions or comment on what they see. You may be able to tell by their facial expression or behavior that they are trying to make sense out of the differences they see, hear, and feel. For example, you may notice a child with a concerned look on her face when she sees a child return after having the chickenpox. She notices the marks and is trying to make sense out of what she sees. A child may be unwilling to hold hands or sit near another child whose behavior or appearance is unusual.

◄o► ◄o► ◄o►

It was Sean's second week in Mrs. Mack's class. Several children already had called him a baby because of his small size. Today Hector came over to Mrs. Mack and said, "Sean is a baby. He's not 3 years old." Mrs. Mack assured Hector, "Oh, yes, Sean is 3 years old." Hector thought for a moment and then announced, "Well! He's not 3 like I'm 3!"

◄o► ◄o► ◄o►

What should Mrs. Mack say? How much explanation is warranted? Should she explain that Sean has Down syndrome? Is his size related to his diagnosis? How can she help the other children understand that he uses sign language to talk? Most importantly, how can she acknowledge that Sean *is* different, but show that he is still an important member of the class? In spite of the differences, she wants to teach *all* the children to appreciate and value each other.

Older children both observe and comment on differences. Some of the first differences they notice are those that are visible. These may be physical abilities, such as the way a person walks or uses his or her hands, or physical characteristics, such as size, facial appearance, or the absence of limbs. As children become more sophisticated, they notice differences in behavior and language, such as frequent temper tantrums, crying, or unusual speech.

Children do not automatically think that differences are bad, but they do ask questions and make comments as they try to understand what they see. They look to the adults around them for signs of how to react. It is up to you, as the teacher, to lead the way. Mrs. Mack has a wonderful opportunity to talk with Hector and the rest of the class, not only about Sean but also about each child's uniqueness. She can help the children talk about differences and similarities and she can help them understand what these differences and similarities mean.

HOW CHILDREN THINK

◄o► ◄o► ◄o►

It was the 4th of July and all the neighborhood families had gathered at the park to watch the fireworks. Trisha's mother noticed her staring at a little boy on the blanket next to them. The little boy didn't have arms and was using his feet to play with toys and eat his dinner. After a while Trisha pulled her arms inside her T-shirt and took off her shoes. She tried to use her feet to play with her toys. Trisha's mother said to her, "I see you noticed that that boy doesn't have arms. He uses his feet really well to eat and play, doesn't he?" Later, on the way home, Trisha commented to her mother, "He really does have arms, doesn't he, Mom? They're just inside his shirt, right?" Trisha was still trying to understand what she saw.

◀◦▶ ◀◦▶ ◀◦▶

When you talk to children about disabilities remember that they do not think like adults. Their questions about disabilities reflect their level of development. They have had fewer experiences in the world that they can use to understand what they see, and they rely on adults to provide them with honest, accurate information.

Some children think that a disability happens because the person did something wrong. For example, a child might think that a person cannot hear because he or she is being punished. You can explain that deafness is not anyone's fault, that it happens when a person's ears do not work. When they see a person with a disability, they may think, "Will it happen to me? Can I catch it? How did that happen?" You can help by saying things such as, "Deafness isn't like a cold. You can't catch it." Young children have a concrete understanding of cause and effect. They relate everything to themselves.

Children have a limited understanding of past and future time and do not understand what "forever" means. Things that happened in the past were "yesterday." Things that will happen are "tomorrow." Everything else is "today" or "later." They may not understand that a disability is permanent. When told that a child is blind and cannot see, they may say, "Well, she'll get to see it tomorrow." Rather than arguing about "forever," it is more important that the child understand about "right now." You might say, "Every day you will see Tameka, but she won't be able to see you."

Even after you answer the questions, children may ask the same question tomorrow or next week. They are trying to understand new ideas that puzzle them, and their understanding changes as they get older. At each new stage of development they need to hear an honest answer that matches their level of understanding.

COMMUNICATING POSITIVE VALUES ABOUT DISABILITIES

The children and adults in your program will follow your example. Be clear about the values you model and teach in your classroom.

- Is diversity welcomed?
- Are differences embraced and celebrated?
- Are each child's unique abilities recognized?
- Are examples of diversity included throughout the classroom in pictures, toys, and books?

In some classrooms a different child is featured each week. A picture is put up on the bulletin board and the child and family share information about themselves during that week.

◄○► ◄○► ◄○►

Christopher brought in his favorite toy and pictures of the whole family including Barney, his dog. His mother read the book, Why Does that Man Have Such a Big Nose? She explained that the book asked a lot of questions about how people look. She said that all people look different from each other. In Christopher's case he would always be very short and he would sometimes need help to reach things, but he was just a kid like them.

◄○► ◄○► ◄○►

Another way to introduce children to people with disabilities is to have classroom visitors who can talk to the children.

◄○► ◄○► ◄○►

Through a special program, Monica, an eighth grader, visited the Montgomery Preschool. She brought her guide dog and talked about what it is like to be blind. She showed the children how she used a cane and her dog to help her find her way around. She answered the children's questions about how she became blind, what she could see, and how she learned where her food was on her plate. The teacher used an activity the next day from the New Friends Curriculum *that let all the children experience what it felt like to be unable to see. She included stories in the library corner about a grandmother who was blind, and she put glasses and a white and red cane in the dress-up corner for the children to use.*

◄○► ◄○► ◄○►

It is important with any awareness activities that the children have a chance to ask questions both at the time of the activity and for several weeks afterward.

Children watch how you react when someone is hurt or teased. Help children verbalize their feelings and think about how others feel. How you behave and the tone of your voice are more important than the specific words you use. Let children know that even though each of them is different, they are all important and valued members of the class. Teach empathy. Children can learn to listen to each other and understand how others feel. As one young girl in the videotape *Regular Lives* explained well, "Just because you can't walk or talk doesn't mean that you don't have feelings!"

Children notice differences all the time. They comment on size, appearance, and behavior. The teacher can acknowledge those comments, provide information, and teach children to become empathetic.

It helps children to get along if they also recognize what they have in common with each other and with the child who has a disability. In class you can talk about everyone who has a baby brother or who likes ice cream. Find common ground to help children see what they share and that a disability is just one part of a person.

This helps children recognize that although they are each different, they are all capable and important. Talk about the things each child does well; then, talk about things that are hard to learn.

Guidelines for Answering
Children's Questions About Differences

Children ask questions about things they can see and experience directly. As a teacher or a parent you probably have been asked difficult questions by children. Children are quite candid and may make comments that surprise you. They also can ask embarrassing questions when you least expect it. Be prepared! Children have inquiring minds and they ask questions to learn about their world. They think about the answers you give them and may come back to you to ask more questions and get more information at a later time. Young children accept simple, factual information. Not responding to a child's questions may lead a child to believe that what he or she asked about should not be discussed or that there is something wrong about the question. For example, if a child in your classroom asks, "What's the matter with her?" simply state, "There's nothing the matter. Amy is not able to walk, so she uses a special chair to get around." You can help all the children understand about a classmate who is blind by explaining that "Miguel's eyes don't work well, so he uses his ears and hands to know where things are." Your answers to the questions are a chance to communicate the positive values discussed in this chapter.

Children absorb information in small doses. They may want a simple explanation without extensive details. Your responses should be direct and simple explanations with examples that they can understand. For instance, a child may ask, "How come he can't talk?" You might answer, "Johnny doesn't talk with words, but he can talk with his hands. Here, let me show you." Another question may be, "How come she's so short?" Your answer might be, "Laurie's body grows more slowly. No one in our class is exactly the same size. We all grow differently."

Use descriptive words that a child will understand. Try to think of an explanation that is something the child might have experienced, for example, "Remember when you wore your earmuffs in the winter and it was hard to hear what I was saying? That is what Jennifer hears most of the time," or "Think about what you see at night. It's dark and you can only see shapes and a little light. That's what seeing is like for Michael."

Look at the expression on a child's face and watch his or her body language, and listen to the tone of his or her voice. Does he or she have a question, but not know how to ask it? Remember that children notice differences even if they do not always talk about them. Children sometimes have a hard time finding the words to express what they are thinking. You may have to ask the questions when you see a child react but not ask. If a child looks fearful and shies away from a person, you might comment, "That man's hand looks scary to you, doesn't it?"

At other times you might see a child staring. This is an opportunity to use the "some children" technique. For example, you can say, "Some children wonder if wearing a brace hurts," or "Some children wonder how you get into a car in a wheelchair. Do you wonder about that?" Then you can provide the answer. You can say, "Sometimes a person has to be picked up and moved into the car and sometimes a person can stand and sit down in the car. Other people have special cars and the wheelchair rolls into the car."

Differences can be frightening or upsetting when they are not understood. You can help by acknowledging and labeling children's reactions, for example, "I noticed you didn't want to sit next to Brian. It scares me when he screams. Does it scare you, too? He needs our help to learn to use words. Let's tell him that his screaming frightens us." In another situation you might say, "I know it makes you sad when Felicia won't play with you, but right now Felicia can't run. She needs to rest. Let's invite her to play after naptime."

Children learn by watching others and noting their reactions. They hear how words are spoken and see how attitudes are demonstrated through facial expression and body language. By being a caring, empathetic teacher, you demonstrate that this is a quality that you value in others. It is a good way to teach children to care about and help each other. "We are going to walk down the hallway in pairs quietly. It helps the children in the other classes to work if we are quiet. Be good friends and remind each other how to walk quietly."

If you understand how children think, the answers you give to their questions provide teaching opportunities for learning about others with sensitivity and caring.

Talking with Parents

You should talk with parents about your program philosophy and curriculum when they enroll their child in your program. Each family has its own values and beliefs and needs to choose a program that is compatible with those values and beliefs. Let parents know that your program does not discriminate against children with disabilities. Provide them with information about inclusion and reassure them that each child gets the time and attention he or she needs. Show them how *all* children benefit by being educated together.

Parents also need to know how to respond to questions or comments that their child might ask at home. Share the information in this chapter with parents. Work with parents so that children learn that their questions will get honest, consistent responses. Be receptive to parents' reports about what their child says about school when he or she is at home.

◄○► ◄○► ◄○►

Mariana Lopez's mother had been really busy with the new baby. She hadn't had time to talk to the preschool teacher because Mariana's father had been taking her to school and a neighbor had been bringing her home. Mariana's teacher, Ms. Jackson, called to ask if Mariana had talked much about her friends at school. Ms. Lopez said, "No, I've been pretty preoccupied lately." Ms. Jackson said that Mariana was usually very friendly to everyone, but recently had been avoiding one of the children in the class. Ms. Jackson explained that this behavior was unusual for Mariana and that the preschool program now included children with disabilities. She was wondering if that was having any effect on Mariana.

Later that night at bedtime, Ms. Lopez asked Mariana about her friends at school. Mariana said immediately, "I don't want to play with Freddy. I don't want to catch what he has. He sounds funny when he talks and makes funny noises." Her mother assured her that she couldn't catch anything from Freddy. It would be fine for her to play with him. He really was just like everyone else even if he looked different. Ms. Lopez called Ms. Jackson the next day and asked her for some suggestions about what to say to Mariana. Ms. Jackson said that she had made a great start. Freddy's mother had asked her to tell the children that Freddy was not sick, but that Freddy learned more slowly than the other children and was still learning to talk. He made strange noises sometimes when he tried to say some new words.

Several days later Ms. Jackson was surprised and pleased to see Mariana joining Freddy at the table for snack.

◄○► ◄○► ◄○►

PRIVACY AND CONFIDENTIALITY

All families have the right to privacy and confidentiality about personal information. It is very important to maintain that confidentiality. Let everyone know that personal information will not be disclosed without specific permission. Although there may be questions about the child with a disability from parents or other staff, classroom staff must not disclose any information about the child unless specific permission has been given by the family. Families should be informed at the time of enrollment that your program is open to all children, including those with special needs.

Parents of children with disabilities have been answering questions about their children since the birth of their children. Ask them for suggestions about how to answer questions and what information they would like others to know about their child.

◄○► ◄○► ◄○►

Before Susan went to kindergarten, her mother Ms. Tracy spoke to the teacher. She wanted to know if the teacher would like her to come to the class and talk to the children about Down syndrome. Mr. Bailey, the teacher, thought that it was a good idea.

About 3 weeks into the school year Ms. Tracy prepared and gave a short talk about Down syndrome and read the children's book Our Brother Has Down Syndrome. *The children were encouraged to ask questions. It soon became clear that the children didn't know that Susan had Down syndrome. The children were more concerned about the fact that Susan was very short and couldn't reach the water fountain. Both Mr. Bailey and Ms. Tracy felt that the discussion with the children was beneficial and allowed them to ask questions openly.*

◄o► ◄o► ◄o►

Some children with disabilities are also used to being asked questions and prefer to give their own answers.

◄o► ◄o► ◄o►

A teacher overheard Jamal asking Stephen why he had physical therapy. Stephen said, "When I was little, I had a stroke and couldn't walk. I had to learn to walk again and therapy gives me exercises to do that."

◄o► ◄o► ◄o►

All children deserve courtesy and respect and should be valued for who they are. Children with disabilities are more alike than different from other children. Teachers can help children value each other by communicating positively about differences, including disabilities, and answering children's questions appropriately.

11

Classroom Strategies

Most teachers and child care providers talk with apprehension about facing the prospect of including a child with a disability in their group. Some teachers and providers are not sure that inclusion is the right thing to do, but most are willing to try. They believe in the philosophy that all children can learn and grow together. Child care providers also look for the professional growth that a new teaching challenge, such as inclusion, can provide. However, they have questions and concerns about their own abilities.

"I have no special training."
"I don't have the skills to work with a child with disabilities."
"Am I going to be responsible for providing special education?"
"Could I hurt the child?"

Even those who believe that inclusion can work, wonder

"Will it take too much time away from the other children?"
"What will the other parents and children say?"
"Will I get support and extra help if I need it?"
"Will the curriculum have to be changed?"

These are all important questions and concerns. The answers to them are not simple.

Each child care provider will have to find the solutions that work best for his or her center, children, and families. Providers may need outside help from parents, the public schools, and other community agencies as they seek the best way to handle this complex situation. Here are some suggestions to guide you as you start this process.

A SOLID FOUNDATION

As you begin to think about including children with disabilities in your classroom, it is important to check that you are using the recommended practices for an early childhood program. Such standards (Figure 1) are good for *all* children and these principles will help you meet increasingly diverse needs. These standards are outlined in a publication by the National Association for the Education of Young Children titled *The What, Why, and How of High-Quality Early Childhood Education: A Guide for On-Site Supervision.*

FIRST STEPS

Several of the previous chapters have talked about the program changes that should be considered as you get ready to serve children with disabilities. Here are some specific ways to prepare the classroom for a child with a disability to make the first 2 weeks go as smoothly as possible.

When any child enrolls in your program, there are forms to complete and enrollment procedures to follow. Your program administrator has now made sure that these procedures do not discriminate against children with disabilities. These same procedures now apply to all the children who enter the center.

Gather Information

The first step in registration should be obtaining the information about the child and family that is necessary for the operation of the center. In addition, it is important to get information that will help the program prepare to meet the child's and family's needs. Many programs have standard forms, such as the Child Profile in Figure 2, which asks parents to provide some developmental information about their child. Specifically, it asks parents to describe their child's likes and dislikes, his or her usual routine, previous group experience, what he or she does when unhappy, and any special precautions and/or other information that could help the center provide the best environment. If you decide to use this form or one like it, it should be used for all children enrolling in your program.

Next, it is important to talk to parents. They are the single, best source of information about their children. Chapters 6 and 8 include specific suggestions for talking with families during the enrollment process. If parents have informed center staff that their child has a disability, ask them to help you plan for their child. When you meet

---

1. The program is based on an understanding of child development.
2. The program is individualized to meet the needs of every child.
3. The physical environment is safe and orderly, containing varied and stimulating toys and materials.
4. Children may select activities and materials that interest them, and they learn by being actively involved.
5. Adults show respect for children's needs and ideas and talk with them in caring ways.
6. Parents feel respected and are encouraged to participate in the program.
7. Staff members have specialized training in early childhood development and education.

Figure 1. Standards of quality programming. (From Koralek, D.G., Colker, L.J., & Dodge, D.T. [1993]. *The what, why, and how of high-quality early childhood education: A guide for on-site supervision.* Washington, DC: National Association for the Education of Young Children; reprinted by permission.)

Child Profile

Please help us know more about your child by telling us about:

Your child's special abilities:

How does he or she communicate (e.g., signing, speaking, eye blinking)?

Names of special people (brothers, sisters, friends):

Your child's favorite toys or playthings:

Your child's favorite foods:

Your child's favorite games, activities, songs:

What scares your child?

What quiets your child when upset?

Activities he or she dislikes:

Things that are hard for him or her:

Other special information or concerns you may wish to share:

Figure 2. The child profile questionnaire. (From Osborne, S., Kniest, B., Garland, C., Moore, D., & Usry, D. [1993]. *Special care curriculum and trainer's manual.* Lightfoot, VA: Child Development Resources; reprinted by permission.)

with parents, ask them if they have information in addition to what they wrote in the Child Profile. See if they can suggest resources to learn about the specific disability. If their child is receiving special education services or is supported by other professionals, such as special educators or therapists, request permission to get information from them. If appropriate, also try to visit the child's special education classroom.

Start slowly and sensitively to build a positive relationship with the parents. Remember to ask open-ended, nonjudgmental questions. Be sensitive to cultural and family values.

James, age 3½, has Down syndrome. His parents met with James's teacher, Sue, to talk about what to expect in the first few days of school.

◄○► ◄○► ◄○►

We explained Down syndrome to Sue and told her that James was talking more but was difficult to understand. James communicated by using sign language, or he could point and take somebody to something he wanted. We gave her a list of the words he knows with pictures of the signs and offered to meet with her to teach her more of James's signs. We assured Sue that James did not have any special physical or medical needs and that we were working very hard on toilet training at home and hoped to coordinate with the school so that James could stop using diapers.

Sue expressed her apprehension. She said she had never known a child with Down syndrome and would like to learn more. We gave her some information to read and the telephone number of James's teacher from last year. We are apprehensive too, but are pleased to be working with the school. We believe this is the best place for James.

◄○► ◄○► ◄○►

Prepare to Answer Questions

Talk to the parents about how they would like you to handle questions that other parents and children in the classroom may ask. You may decide to do some awareness activities about disabilities with your children before the arrival of a child with a disability. Chapter 4 provides information and suggestions about that topic.

Before James's first day, Sue spent some time talking with the children in her class about disabilities.

◄○► ◄○► ◄○►

I read the group a story about a child with Down syndrome that had a lot of pictures. I also found the Sesame Street Sign Language Fun *book to teach everyone a few signs, and I added a song in sign language to the morning circle. In addition, I added a new job to the job chart—class helper. The class helper is going to be a friend who will lend a "helping hand" to other children when they need it.*

◄○► ◄○► ◄○►

Plan a Transition

If possible, have the new child visit the classroom before he or she starts full time. Some children do best with a gradual transition that includes short visits with their parents. Some children do better with immediate full-time attendance. The transition plan and classroom visits should be discussed with the family and guided by the needs of the child.

James's mother brought him to visit the school.

I stayed in the classroom for just a few minutes and then waited in the office for a while. James joined the class for group time and snack. He seemed to have a great time.

Make the Child Welcomed

For any child, starting a new group program can be difficult. It is important for you, as the teacher, to think of ways to make the new child feel welcome and help him get to know the other children. James's teacher tells about his first week.

James started school the next week. My new "class helper," Tawanda, took James around the classroom and showed him where his cubby was. She also helped him put his things away and showed him where to sit at snack. During our morning circle, all the children introduced themselves and we gave James a card we had made to welcome him to our group. At first, some of the children didn't want to hold his hand or play with him. But by the end of the week, two children had become good friends with James. They had learned several signs and could even tell me what he wanted.

It Isn't Easy

In spite of the best plans and preparation, everything may not go smoothly in the classroom. It is a time of change. Expect that having a child with a disability may sometimes be hard work. Ask your administrator to be on call in case you need extra help during the first few days. Remember, you are not solely responsible for including a child with a disability. It should be a team effort involving the teacher, parents, administrators, and other community professionals. James's teacher talks about her feelings.

I really worked hard that first week—maybe it was the extra anxiety. I was so afraid I would do something wrong and I didn't want to harm James. But James's mother called or stayed after school to answer my questions each day. James's special education teacher also visited one morning and gave me some helpful tips and took some ideas back to her classroom. Jane, my director, stopped in several times each morning and helped me take the children to the bathroom and get them ready to go outside. By the end of the week I felt that things would work out. I felt I had really accomplished something and I was proud of the way the children had accepted James. Even though I don't know a lot about Down syndrome, I think James is a neat kid and I know I can teach him.

◄o► ◄o► ◄o►

When You Can't Prepare

If a child's entrance into the program is sudden, you will not have time to "get ready." In this situation, it is important to get administrative and parent support as soon as possible. Speak up for yourself and the other children if you think that a potentially dangerous situation has been created. Try to follow the same process of gathering information, learning about the disability, and developing positive social interactions between the new child and his or her classmates. Again, try to be flexible, do the best you can, and ask for the support you need.

On Monday morning, Denise, the teacher of the 3-year-olds class is told she will have a new student that day—Clara, age 3½, who has spina bifida. Denise has a lot of questions, but the director has to deal with a crisis and disappears.

◄o► ◄o► ◄o►

When Clara's mother arrived to drop Clara off, she stayed a minute to introduce herself and give me a box of diapers and a change of clothes. She told me, "Treat Clara just like any other child in the class. I don't want any special treatment for her. She'll do fine if she knows you mean it. This is her walker. She needs it to get around."

At this point, I really started to get worried. I knew nothing about spina bifida, and I had never met Clara before. My assistant was absent and I had a new substitute. Another child in the group, Mary, who just started last week, still cries at the door when her mother leaves. Thank heavens I have taught for 5 years. I decided that what has worked for me before in the classroom will work with Clara.

It was a long morning. Some of the children made fun of Clara because she couldn't walk. The other children ignored her. She wet through her diaper and when I left the room to change her, Mary screamed because she thought I was leaving. Clara wouldn't listen at group time, she tried to take the other children's snacks, and she tried to crawl out of the room several times.

I was exhausted. I'm really worried because Clara just doesn't fit in. She behaves more like the 2-year-olds I used to teach. I'm surprised and disappointed that the other children teased her, but I don't know if I should talk to them about Clara's disability. I'm really angry at my director for not telling me about Clara's enrollment sooner.

I decided to keep my concerns to myself. When the other staff members asked how it had gone, I smiled and said, "Fine, no problem." If I complain, they'll think I'm a bad teacher. I decided not to speak to my director because I don't want to lose my temper or appear prejudiced or intolerant of a child with a disability. I'll just give it a few more days, but I know I can't do this forever. If I have to, I'll quit.

◄o► ◄o► ◄o►

Poor Denise and Clara! Below is a summary of some do's and don'ts for preparing for a new child in the classroom. Try to apply some of them to change the picture for Denise and Clara.

The following is a list of some do's in preparing for a new child in the classroom:

- Talk to the parents in advance.
- Gather information about the child and the disability.
- Establish open communication with all involved; ask questions and express concerns freely.
- Plan carefully for the child's first day.
- Talk to the class about disabilities and prepare the children for any new child.
- Have the child visit the classroom.
- Have someone to call on for immediate assistance.
- Expect some bad days.

The following is a list of some don'ts in preparing for a new child in the classroom:

- Be afraid to ask parents questions about their child.
- Be afraid to admit you don't know.
- Try to do everything yourself.
- Criticize children for noticing and asking questions about disabilities.
- Hesitate to express your concerns.
- Dismiss your own and your children's fears and anxieties about disabilities.
- Hesitate to question the placement.
- Expect everything to go smoothly the first day.
- Be surprised if you work harder at first.
- Expect to make the child "normal."

Short-Term Strategies

You need to review your daily schedule and decide what times of the day or events in the day require the most adult assistance. Talk to your administrator and see if he or she can find extra help for you during those times of the day on a short-term basis (2–4 weeks). Could you arrange for an additional person, volunteer, or paid staff person who could provide assistance during the first few days?

Keep in mind that there is an adjustment period for all new children entering the program. Whether a child begins a part-time or full-time transition will make a difference. The length of adjustment varies from child to child. In the case of a child with a disability, this period may last a little longer and require more patience. It also may be prolonged if it takes awhile to find and make the necessary classroom adaptations.

Be prepared to make daily adjustments in your schedule, curriculum, and physical environment as you get to know the child.

Long-Term Strategies

One of the goals of a high-quality, early childhood program is that the teacher is expected to try to meet each child's needs. This is a very challenging task that becomes even more demanding as the diversity of children in the classroom increases. How do you meet diverse needs effectively and make sure that no one is overlooked? The adaptations for one child must not jeopardize the learning of any other child. Many of the most helpful strategies can be developed only after you get to know the child and he or she has spent some time in your classroom. The ideas presented here are not comprehensive. Consider them guidelines for general areas of classroom practice. The ability to meet each child's needs is often dependent on the creativity and resourcefulness of the classroom teacher.

As you begin to adapt the classroom for children with disabilities, remember three important concepts—access, usability, and maximized learning. Can the child physically get where he or she needs to be in the classroom to learn something? Once the child is in that location, are the materials usable and can the child participate in the activity as independently as possible to learn something? Are the learning activities arranged and scheduled to meet the individual learning needs of the children, including the child with disabilities? Are the learning activities adapted to maximize independence in learning? These are questions you should ask about the environment and the materials in your room.

Changing the Environment

Infants need very secure environments that will allow them to use their senses and explore. One of the most important factors in an infant environment is a consistent caregiver. Toddlers need a balance of security and independence. They still rely on their senses for most of their learning, but they are driven to move and being able to use their bodies in the environment is very important. They are so mobile, in fact, that the caregiver needs to be able to see all areas of the room at once. Preschoolers need well-organized, clearly defined classrooms with areas that promote independence, foster decision making, and encourage initiative and involvement. These areas need not only to be attractive and inviting, but also must lend themselves to use by small groups in order to foster social competence.

You will know when the environment is not working by the behavior of the children. Infants become fussy and restless from being in one place too long away from toys or interesting things to watch and touch. Toddlers fight over toys, run around the room aimlessly, and begin clammering for the caregiver's attention all at once. Preschoolers seem bored and unengaged. They wander around looking for something to do or are dependent on adults to tell them what to do.

Children with disabilities need the same things in their classroom environments as other children. They need an environment that is safe and secure and provides activities and materials for their development. When a child with a disability has different developmental needs than children of the same age, then adaptations must be made. For example, a teacher might expect a toddler to trip and fall many times during the day as he or she is learning to walk, so furniture is arranged with wide spaces between it and more open space to move in. This helps prevent bumps and bruises. If a child of 3 or 4 has balance problems and is likely to fall often, similar arrangements in the classroom furniture may need to be made. If falling is likely because of a disability, a child may have to wear a helmet, similar to the ones used in cycling, to protect his or her head from serious injury.

Infant and toddler classrooms also have quiet, comfortable spaces for children to go when they become agitated or upset. It is a place that they can go alone or with the adult of their choice that feels good physically; it can be a lap, a rocking chair, a swing, or a special place in the room. Children need this part of the environment to help calm themselves. They are not always developmentally able to tell the caregiver what they need or what is bothering them. A teacher might expect a 3- or 4-year-old who is more verbally adept to "talk" his or her problems out. However, a child who has language difficulties and cannot talk about being upset still needs a secure place in the classroom to be alone or with the person of his or her choice in order to calm down. Many preschool classrooms have quiet corners that usually house books or tape recorders with headphones. An adaptation could be to occasionally designate this place for one child at a time if someone needs a quiet area to calm down and get over being upset. Adaptations require either adding something to the environment that is not already there or using something in the environment in a different way.

Equipment and Materials Equipment and materials in the environment should be flexible enough so that they can be used by children with a range of abilities. Blocks, sand, and water tables can suit children of many developmental levels. For any age child, the equipment and materials should foster independence. For toddlers, equipment also needs to support motor development. Preschoolers need materials invitingly displayed with visual cues about how and where to use them—for example, areas defined by tape on the floor to show where to build with the blocks and pictures of block constructions. Of course, all equipment and materials should support the development of new concepts and skills in children with diverse developmental levels.

The addition of a child with physical disabilities to your group may require some special equipment. Such equipment might include

- Chairs to help a child sit better (e.g., a corner chair or a bolster chair with head and back support)
- A standing apparatus for a child who cannot stand alone (e.g., a prone stander)
- Wheelchairs
- Body, hand, or leg braces that keep the trunk, arms, and legs in good positions or help make limbs more functional

Ask the child's parents for an explanation of the equipment to help you learn when and how it is to be used. The child's parents can demonstrate what needs to be done and you can try it yourself while the parents are observing. Check to see if the child's physical or occupational therapist can consult with you about the use of the equipment. If you are uncomfortable with using the equipment, keep working with the parents, ask for clarification, and try different alternatives until the best situation for you and the child has been found. Write down the procedures if equipment and use is complicated.

Children with hearing or language impairments also may need special devices. Some children may need hearing aids or amplifiers. Language boards and augmentative or alternative communication devices can help other children communicate about what they want and help conversations. Again, ask the parents to explain and demonstrate the devices. Also ask for guidance about their use from the child's speech-language therapist or audiologist.

Often the largest pieces of equipment in the classroom are the furniture. One of the most important things you can do for a child with physical disabilities is to make sure that he or she has enough room to maneuver in the room. For a child who has a visual impairment, you need to keep large furniture in the same place. Prepare all the children for room changes or include them in the planning of the changes. If the furniture or room arrangement is going to change, make sure that the child with a visual impairment gets to explore and learn the new arrangement.

For children with hearing impairments, the environment needs to include additional clear and noticeable visual cues to help them function independently and understand what is happening in the classroom. For example, you can flick the lights to signal an activity change, rather than ringing a bell. Use manual signs as you sing the song for cleanup time.

Tactile cues help children who have visual impairments locate equipment and materials. The name on the child's cubby can be marked with a textured sign that the child can feel. Small manipulatives can be taped on the outside of bins to help the child identify where each piece of equipment belongs.

As children come into your room, they will let you know by their actions and sometimes their words what other equipment and materials should be added or changed in your room. Toddlers really do not share toys well. If they always seem to be quarreling over a favorite toy, you need to add several more of the same toy. When older children begin to build more sophisticated constructions with the blocks and run out of blocks before they are finished, see if you can add another set. To act out a story that you have read, change the "dress-up" clothes to match the story.

The Daily Schedule

Planning for Typical Children   The schedule for infants is very flexible and is determined by the needs of each individual child. The routine is centered around caregiving such as feeding, diapering, and sleeping. The toddler schedule also is flexible; play times become longer, and sleep and care demands decrease. Short activity periods are interspersed with caregiving routines. Changing activities and moving from place to place for this age group take a lot of time. The preschool schedule has planned events that reflect the needs, interests, and abilities of the children. There is a balance between active and quiet time periods, child-initiated and teacher-directed events, and individual small and large group activities. The consistent structure and routines provide security to children in this age group. Events are scheduled so that each child has time for playing, eating, resting, learning, and interacting with others.

Planning for Children with Special Needs   Until recently, the classroom routine for children with disabilities was developed with a primary focus on the limitations in learning that resulted from the disability. It included more direct teaching in one-on-one situations with practice and drill in simulated situations using behavioral principles. This sometimes resulted in children learning skills that did not transfer to other situations inside and outside of the classroom. For example, a child might learn to button on a board, but then be unable to transfer the learning to his or her coat, or children might learn to sort circles, squares, and triangles but were unable to sort knives, spoons, and forks. In special education classrooms, learning times were organized to address delayed or absent skills in specific learning domains. Children completed the same tasks repeatedly (e.g., naming pictures of objects). Such activities may not be very motivating and in some cases are not developmentally appropriate. These teaching strategies stemmed from efforts to fulfill goals and the behavioral objectives to a specific criterion level stipulated in individualized education programs. Special education teachers have been accountable for ensuring learning through carefully planned activities and documented progress.

Special education classrooms for young children are currently undergoing change. In part, this has been a growing recognition of developmentally appropriate practice (Bredekamp, 1987). There now is more effort to plan activities that are real, not artificially developed, and functional, and to use natural environments for learning activities. The events in the classroom are changing to reflect what children without disabilities at similar developmental levels are learning and doing. The skills that children learn in these settings are now selected because they are important to children in a variety of settings—in school, at home, and in the community—and they promote the enjoyment of learning. Some children with disabilities will still need more opportunities to practice newly acquired skills.

Labeling the Environment Environmental cues for identifying a scheduled event might include pictures or labels for the center, library, music, blocks, housekeeping, manipulatives, or art. You also could put pictures or labels on the shelves indicating what is stored in each location. An event or schedule sequence could be used to provide cues to let the children know what is expected of them.

Modifying the Schedule As you adjust your routines to include children with disabilities, think about the events in your daily schedule in terms of the following characteristics: structure, grouping, activity level, time, purpose, and the role of the teacher. You can then make adjustments based on each child's needs and level of development.

As you begin to adapt your schedule for children with disabilities, ask yourself these general questions:

- Is there a schedule that is predictable for the children and reflects little "down" or waiting time?
- Is the classroom schedule flexible enough to accommodate programming changes?
- Are the blocks of time in the classroom schedule developmentally appropriate for the group?
- How and when do children move from one activity to the next? Is there a clear signal or do they have to wait any length of time to begin the next activity?
- How will you provide access to special program events, such as field trips?

For each child with a disability, consider whether she does well in child-initiated activities or could benefit from more teacher direction. Can the child work in large groups or does she need more individualized attention? What is the child's activity level tolerance? And finally, what level of independence does the child show during transitions and waiting times? Does the child understand the cues for activity changes?

When a child care situation has children with variable schedules, such as in an infant care situation, it is not difficult to include the child with special needs.

Selene is a 10-month-old child with Down syndrome. She just started in a Mother's Day Out program at the church. After a few visits, her mother asked the teacher how Selene was doing.

◀◉▶ ◀◉▶ ◀◉▶

Hi, I was wondering how Selene is adjusting. The teacher told her, "We really have a flexible schedule here. The children are all under 18 months of age, and they all have a different time clock. Selene has fit right in. The only thing we've noticed is that she needs some help rolling back to her stomach. She will flip over and then complain. We help her practice rolling onto her stomach. She's just about got it."

◀◉▶ ◀◉▶ ◀◉▶

Some children have different needs that require schedule adjustments and new skills from the caregiver.

Ethan is a 22-month-old child who was very premature. He just started in a toddler room at a neighborhood child care center. He crawls, but does not walk yet, and is fed with a gastrostomy tube. His father called his teacher to make sure that he was adjusting all right.

◀◉▶ ◀◉▶ ◀◉▶

Oh, Ethan's doing great! He has such a sunny disposition. My assistant and I are still nervous with the G-tube feedings, but I think we will get the hang of it. We've had to adjust the lunch schedule because sometimes his feedings take a long time. We start Ethan before the others sit down. Because he has to sit upright for an hour before taking his nap, he is the last to go to sleep. Also, I want to let you know that we wanted to give Ethan the freedom to crawl, but were afraid he would get trampled. During really busy times like toileting and hand washing, he sits in his special chair near one of us so we can talk to him. We also are trying a Kiddie Corral that the director got that we can move around to different parts of the room. It protects Ethan and he can crawl to different shelves. We usually have another quiet child play there, too. I was worried that it might look like a cage because I really don't like playpens. Please stop in and tell me what you think or if you have any other ideas.

◀◉▶ ◀◉▶ ◀◉▶

Sometimes adaptations require trial and error and continued adjustments to find the right schedule.

Justin, a very active child with a visual impairment, attends his neighborhood preschool. At first Ms. Clark, his teacher, was concerned because she had never worked with a child like him. She talked to his mother and did some reading. She set up the classroom and had his mother help introduce him to the areas of the room. She used very bright tape to mark different areas. She also added a fuzzy sticker to Justin's cubby, carpet square, and chair so he could find them.

After the first 2 weeks, Ms. Clark talked to her director.

◄o► ◄o► ◄o►

Justin's vision is the least of my worries. Justin seems very bright and can figure out his own cues for where he is and what is happening. He just can't seem to handle the schedule. The children are used to playing for long periods of time on their own without help from me. They know when it is time to change activities and what will happen next. Justin just doesn't seem to understand.

◄o► ◄o► ◄o►

After some suggestions from the director, Ms. Clark made a few adjustments.

◄o► ◄o► ◄o►

I made a schedule board with tactile cues so that Justin could make a plan for his one long play time and could refer back to it on his own. I also added more small group times and kept Justin with the same group of children for 2 weeks. They were good about helping him stay on task. I gave Justin his own timer so that he would have a few minutes of extra warning before it was time to change activities. His day isn't completely smoothed out, but it's getting there.

◄o► ◄o► ◄o►

Well-planned and balanced schedules give children the security and predictability to function independently and maximize learning throughout the day.

ACTIVITY ADAPTATION AND INDIVIDUALIZATION FOR EACH CHILD

The same activity may be used with a group of children and can be adapted if all of the children have similar learning needs or if some children have different learning needs. As a caregiver, you already make adaptations every day for the children in your group. You will use the same process to make adaptations for children with disabilities. Determine the learning goal and purpose of the activity and then ask the following questions:

- Does the curriculum allow for individualized teaching with flexibility to meet a variety of learning needs?
- Do the materials need to be changed? In a cutting activity, should you have different types of scissors? Do you need right-handed scissors and left-handed scissors, squeeze scissors, blunt or pointed scissors? Do you need simple shapes or complex shapes? Stiff paper or thin paper?
- How much time will the activity take? Can some children do it quickly and some do it slowly?

- Does everyone have to do the activity? Does everyone have to do it at the same time?
- If the activity has many steps, how should it be broken down for teaching? Can the children do the whole activity independently? How much help will they need? How can it be simplified?
- For children with visual and auditory impairments, can the directions be both demonstrated and verbal?

Figure 3 is an example of one activity that can be adapted to meet the different learning needs of children.

Figure 4 is another example of an activity that can be adapted to meet the different learning needs of children. The same analysis can be applied to activities that teach other skills from the curriculum (Figure 5).

Children with disabilities also may have very specific learning goals in the individualized education programs or family service plans (see Chapter 4). Some teachers may wish to reinforce the spe-

---

Choice or Free Play Time

Structure: Child-initiated
Grouping: Individual
Activity level: Active to quiet
Time: 45–60 minutes
Purpose:
1. Involve children actively in learning through play.
2. Provide opportunity for choice.

Role of Teacher:
1. Help children make a plan.
2. Observe children.
3. Participate in play and serve as a model.
4. Encourage interaction among children.
5. Assist children who are having difficulty with materials or other children.
6. Help children clean up.

Figure 3.   Plan for a child-initiated play time. (Adapted from Abraham, Morris, & Wald [1993].)

Goal: Identifying shapes (e.g., knives, forks, spoons)
Task/activity: Sorting plastic utensils to set the table in the housekeeping corner
  I. **Same goal, same task**
      All children sort utensils into three piles.
  II. **Same goal, same task (task adapted)**
      Some children are given larger utensils that are easier to grasp and distinguish visually.
  III. **Same goal, different task**
      Some children match utensils to pictures or use a drawer organizer box that has shaped slots for utensils.
  IV. **Different goal, different task**
      Some children are given one fork, knife, and spoon to hold up when the utensil is asked for by name.

Figure 4.   Adapting a sorting activity.

cial education goals by using some of the same learning goals and activities in the child care curriculum. Figure 6 is an example of a form one teacher used to highlight learning events in her schedule and remind the classroom staff of an individual child's learning goals and activities.

Because you use many different activities and teach many different children, you will have to be flexible. Some ideas can be gen-

---

Goal: Sequencing (events)

Task/activity: Story time

I. Same goal, same task

Teacher tells a story using a flannel board. A child repeats the story using a flannel board.

II. Same goal, same task (task adapted)

Teacher tells a story using a flannel board. Teacher repeats the story and a child puts the pieces on the flannel board while the story is told.

III. Same goal, different task

Teacher tells a story using a flannel board. Children draw a picture from memory of some of the story characters.

IV. Different goal, different task

Teacher tells a story using a flannel board. Children point to characters when the teacher names them.

Figure 5. Adapting a sequencing activity.

ACTIVITY AREAS OF ROOM
Activities from IEP/IFSP to Be Facilitated by Staff

Teacher's name: __Mrs. Tores__   Child: __Malik__   Date: __7/29/94__

Please help <u>Malik</u> with the following:

HOUSEKEEPING
• Follow one-step direction to 10.

BOOK
• Turn one page at a time.
• Point to familiar objects.

CIRCLE
• Participate with group.
• Ask for a song or book.

BLOCK AREA
• Stack a variety of objects.

TABLE ACTIVITIES
• Complete four-piece puzzle.
• String large beads.

ART
• Cut on a line with scissors.
• Manipulate Play-Doh.

Comments:

1. Malik should wear his braces all day. Please check them at noon and before he goes home.
2. Do not let him W-sit. He can sit with his legs out straight, legs bent and crossed in front, or in a chair.

Figure 6. Integrating the IEP into the curriculum. (From Coleman, C. [1993]. *Integrating IEP goals into daily classroom activities.* South Hill, VA: Author.)

erated on the spot. Some will take more time to determine. Enlist parents, your colleagues, and the children to help you with the task.

Before making activity adaptations for children with disabilities

- Give yourself and the child time to adjust.
- Assume the child is able to participate in **all** activities.
- Watch the child during activities. See what he or she can do and what areas may need adaptation.
- Make adaptations after you have met and gotten to know the child.
- Try to arrange some back-up support during the first week or so for activities that need a lot of teacher direction.

Well-conceived activities are

- Flexible enough to meet a variety of developmental learning needs for individualization
- Able to meet multiple learning objectives
- Motivating and interesting to the children

Behaviors of Concern and Transitions

When children display behaviors of concern in the classroom, it is important to refer back to the behavioral expectations of a child of that age. For example, biting is an often-cited problem in group care. But biting by a 2-year-old is viewed differently than the biting behavior of a 4- or 5-year-old. The expectations for an older child are quite different.

Remember that desired behaviors can be taught just as skills in other developmental areas. If a child has difficulty cutting, watch how the child performs the cutting task and analyze what needs to be taught. Perhaps break down the task, teach the steps, and give the child plenty of opportunities to apply and practice what is taught. Teaching positive behavior requires the same observation, analysis, careful guidance, and opportunities to practice. To help children learn appropriate ways to behave, you must use the same good teaching skills that you use to teach skills in the language, cognitive, and motor areas. Directions and activities that are clear and appropriate for the child's developmental level and your consistent and nurturing presence as the child tackles the new skill will help children learn.

What are the characteristics of behavior? *Behavior* is a reaction or response related to people or the environment. It is observable and measurable. It is patterned, stable, and predictable. Most important, behavior is meaningful to the child. He or she is telling you something by doing the only thing he or she knows how to do and because it makes sense to him or her.

- Jeremy is rolling on the floor kicking and yelling, "No, no, no!"
- Letitia keeps jumping up from circle time and going to the dollhouse.

- Matthew cuts awkwardly around a shape, and halfway through it he throws down the scissors and tears up his paper.
- Several children are making collages and are crowded around a small container of glue. Two of them begin pulling on the glue bowl and it spills on the floor.

Are all these children misbehaving?

The following example describes a problem that one child care provider faced.

◄◦► ◄◦► ◄◦►

It is now the third week of working with my new group. I was used to working with 3-year-olds so moving to the kindergarten was quite an adjustment. Although I have seen the children before, because we are all in the same building, I was still surprised that they were so independent and knew so much. My extra planning has paid off and almost all the children are getting adjusted to the schedule. I do continue to worry about Jeremy. He refuses to stop his activity and clean up. When the other children try to help him by putting the toys away, he starts hitting them. He has had several tantrums when it is time to come in from the playground. I just don't understand it because he is very cooperative the rest of the time.

◄◦► ◄◦► ◄◦►

Jeremy may need extra time to prepare for a change of activities. His teacher could help by reviewing the schedule at the beginning of the day and providing a warning before the change in activity.

Behavior is communication just like spoken language. Your job is to figure out what the child is "saying." Do you need to change anything in the physical environment, activities, or social environment? A child's behavior is always telling the teacher something. Maybe he or she has not learned how to behave or what is expected. She might want attention or he might want more control in the situation. It is often difficult to know what the message is, but the teacher can shape and support more desirable behavior. How is that done? How do you teach it?

Preventive Strategies

Here are some ways you can prevent problems using the same principles that you use to teach other developmental skills.

Tell   Tell and remind the child the rules for the classroom and how he or she is expected to behave. Set reasonable limits for the child. These limits should

- Be the smallest number possible
- Be enforceable
- Have clear consequences
- Be consistent (always acceptable or always not acceptable)

For example, "In our classroom, we follow directions, share toys, keep hands and feet to ourselves, and walk inside the school. In our classroom, we do *not* throw materials, hit or kick others, or run inside."

These rules can be taught formally at circle time. Have everyone identify their feet and their hands. Talk about where they belong and what kinds of things they should be doing. "I can keep my hands and feet to myself. I can use my hands for clapping and building. I can use my feet for walking, kicking a ball, and tiptoeing." Role play with a puppet that has hands and feet. The puppet tries to put his hands and feet on one of the children. The children practice telling the puppet, "Keep hands and feet to self."

Preschool-age children also can be involved in making rules and problem solving difficult situations. Post the rules with pictures and make your expectations clear. Give reminders when necessary.

In a kindergarten classroom the children knew that one of the rules was to share materials. When the new paint boxes arrived, it was hard to decide who should get one.

◄○► ◄○► ◄○►

Yesterday when I brought out the new paint boxes, the children argued about who should get a new one. I decided to have a discussion with the children and see if they could help me solve the problem. I asked them, "Who should get the new paint boxes?" One little girl said, "All the girls should get new paint boxes." The boys said, "No, that's not fair!" I said, "How about drawing x's and o's on pieces of paper and picking like we do for jobs. The o's get new paint boxes tomorrow and the x's get new paint boxes today." Kevin added, "And there should be no complaining." They drew slips of paper and settled the situation amicably. I really was pleased that the children had helped to solve the problem and learned the important social skill of negotiation.

◄○► ◄○► ◄○►

Model Show the children ways to use materials and interact with other people. The teacher is a live demonstration of the type of behavior that should be seen in the classroom. If the teacher uses a very loud voice or sits on the table, it makes it difficult for the children to understand why they cannot do the same thing. Make sure that you praise children who are behaving well and point out that behavior to the others. For example, "Jennifer has found the pots and pans. She's very busy cooking and having a wonderful time. Good for you. That looks delicious, Jennifer."

Plan Structure the environment, the daily routine, and transition times so that they are predictable and consistent for the children. When the children know what to expect, they will feel safe and comfortable.

Transition Transition is the time involved in changing from one activity or location to the next. Very often in classrooms, cleanup time or waiting in line are transition times; children are ending one activity and starting another. Some children may finish before others and have to wait. Children may have difficulty waiting. If they do have difficulty waiting, try to

- Have a consistent routine.
- Cut down the number of changes children have to make.
- Eliminate waiting time.
- Be prepared to start the next activity quickly.
- Find ways children can participate actively (e.g., singing the clean-up song).
- Tell children or show them pictures of what will happen next.

You should think about activities you can use during transition times and plan for them just like other events in the daily schedule. If you know that children must wait to go to lunch while everyone washes hands and uses the bathroom, have books to look at or sing songs and do finger plays with the children who are waiting.

Intervention Strategies

When undesirable or problem behavior continues to occur, try to analyze the behavior systematically and use specific strategies to change behavior. It may help to describe and write down information about the situation. Table 1 is an example of a format that can be used to organize the information.

There are several strategies you can use that help shape positive behavior.

Purposely Ignoring   It is okay to ignore a behavior if you believe that calling attention to it may make it worse, it is not hurting or bothering the other children, or it is helping the child in some way. If the behavior is one that demands attention, such as calling the teacher's name and interrupting, ignoring the child will cause the behavior to increase before it decreases.

Table 1.   Sample behavior description format

Behavior of concern	What is behavior communicating?	Desired behavior	What can be changed?
Pinching	The child next to me is too close.	Talking	1. Arrange play areas to allow children enough space. 2. Help children use their words to express feelings. 3. Help children choose play areas that are less crowded.
Grabbing toys	I want what he or she has.	Sharing, turn taking	1. Have more than one of the most popular toy. 2. Choose toys that two or more can play with. 3. Help children learn to take turns. For example, a child can have a toy for 3 minutes and then give it to the next child for 3 minutes.

◄o► ◄o► ◄o►

Timmy puts fingers in his mouth and twirls his hair around a finger while he waits his turn to speak in circle. I have decided not to say anything to him because I have noticed that it seems to calm him and helps him listen to the other children. I'm going to try giving him objects to hold or small helping jobs at circle, like holding the flannel board piece, so that he can learn to use his hands in more appropriate ways.

◄o► ◄o► ◄o►

Redirecting   When you see a child headed for trouble, you can often stop behavior before it happens and redirect the child's attention.

◄o► ◄o► ◄o►

I saw Jimmy pick up a block and start to throw it. I was able to say, "Let's build a big tower. Bring your block over here, Jimmy," before it actually happened.

◄o► ◄o► ◄o►

Offering Appropriate Choices   Sometimes a child will refuse to cooperate because he or she is seeking control of the situation. You can provide two choices of appropriate ways the child can do the task.

◄o► ◄o► ◄o►

At clean-up time when I asked Jill to put the blocks away, she said, "No." Next time I will try to remember to ask, "Jill, do you want to put the blocks or the Legos away?" Maybe giving Jill a chance to make a choice will help her cooperate.

◄o► ◄o► ◄o►

Explaining Natural/Logical Consequences   Respond to the behavior in ways that make sense to the child in light of the situation. Consequences that are connected and concrete will make sense to young children.

◄o► ◄o► ◄o►

Melvin was having trouble at the sandbox. I stood next to him and asked, "What is the rule about playing in the sandbox? That's right, the sand should stay low. Melvin, I saw you throwing sand up in the air and it got in Elaine's eye. That hurts a lot. The sandbox is closed for you now. Let's find something else for you to do now and you can try the sandbox tomorrow."

◄o► ◄o► ◄o►

Removing from Social Situation   Sometimes a child needs to be removed from the situation so he or she can regain control and settle down. This should be done calmly but firmly and without anger.

Penelope loves to play in the sand. Today she got very excited and started to throw it. I told her to sit with me on the steps. I asked her if she remembered the sandbox rules. She told me, "Sand stays in the sandbox and children don't throw sand." We agreed that she would go back and use the sand to make castles. I stayed with her until she was busily engaged in her construction.

Serious and Persistent Behaviors

There are some children who have more serious and persistent behaviors that can injure themselves or others. Examples of these are self-stimulatory behaviors, such as rocking, hand flapping, and teeth grinding. Other examples are self-injurious behaviors such as head banging, eye poking, and biting one's arms. These behaviors are quite difficult to handle. Occasionally, you will have children with severe emotional problems who can be extremely aggressive or destructive.

Some of these serious behaviors are caused by physiological needs in the child. Eye poking is often seen in children who are blind. These children may experience some visual stimuli from the pressure in an ordinarily deprived sense. Children who have metabolic disorders, such as Lesch-Nyhan syndrome, engage in self-injurious behavior as a result of their organic dysfunction. It is almost impossible to completely stop behaviors from organic causes. It is also very difficult to understand what the child is trying to communicate because these behaviors often occur in children who are nonverbal. If the child becomes upset or angry, you may see an increase in these behaviors.

In such cases the teacher needs to ask several important questions.

- Does the behavior interfere with learning and socialization?
- Is the child or others at risk for injury?
- Does it interfere with the learning of others by distracting or upsetting them?
- How often do I see this specific behavior?
- In what situations or settings does the behavior occur?
- How intense is the behavior? Does it look worse than it is? Is gentle pressure being applied, or is actual damage taking place?
- How long does the behavior last? Has it been happening for a long time? Do you expect it to continue, or is it related to a specific activity or event? For example, is the child under stress as a result of illness or problems at home?

When such behaviors occur, it is important to get assistance in handling them. These behaviors are so resistant to change that you must respond consistently wherever the child is. Ask the parents what they do and what they feel is appropriate for you to do in your program. If the child has a special behavior program, ask for the program and assistance in learning how to use the program properly. If the child has a behavior specialist working with him or her, ask if that person can consult with your program or seek a specialist to help you in your program. Do not try to take on this task alone. A child care program's first responsibility is to the well-being of the children and staff.

There are things you can do that can be very effective with serious behaviors. You must do them very systematically with precision and consistency. One way to handle aggressive behavior is to teach the child the appropriate way to do something and the situation in which the behavior can be used. Instead of kicking other children or furniture, teach them to play soccer or kick ball. Instead of hitting others, suggest the child use a punching balloon. Another way to handle some of the behaviors is to teach him or her alternative or incompatible behaviors. For example, if a child is busily engaged in playing with a toy (e.g., a finger puppet) that requires the use of his or her hands, then the child cannot hit or flap his or her hands or poke others' eyes. Sometimes these children simply have very few skills and need to learn new ways to use their hands and feet. Help them learn to dance instead of kick or use words instead of bite.

CRISIS MANAGEMENT

Once in a while you may encounter a situation in which children are in immediate danger. The following are some crisis management techniques you can use.

1. *Stop the aggression*   An adult intervenes and stops the aggressive or destructive behavior. The adult then separates the children if more than one child is involved.
2. *Remove the disruptive child*   An adult removes the disruptive child and directs the child to a certain chair, quiet corner, or an out-of-the-way place.
3. *Attend to the hurt child*   An adult praises the hurt child for remaining calm, following rules, and focusing on work and play.
4. *Calmly restate the expectations to the disruptive child*   An adult must be brief. This is not a time for teaching or discussing. Use simple direct language such as, "There is no hitting," not "How many times have I told you not to hit because it hurts and makes the other children cry and I get mad." Tell the child how you want him or her to behave. Direct the child's attention to the rules, and use visual cues if it helps the child to understand.
5. *Allow "get yourself together" time*   An adult helps the disruptive child to relax. If it helps, model the following "relaxation" strategies:
    • Take a few deep breaths.

- Move your shoulders up, then down.
- Stop and wait, or stop and think.
- Take a short walk in the hallway.
- Squeeze your hands. Squeeze my hands.
- Stamp your feet.
- Relax your muscles—be a rag doll.
- Say something to yourself, or slowly count to five to yourself. Talk about ways that you see the child is relaxing (e.g., "Your legs are quiet, you are breathing slowly.")

6. *Support the disruptive child*   An adult supports the child when he or she re-enters the classroom activity and stays with the child until he or she is engaged in constructive activity.

7. *Choose a calming activity*, such as the listening center. A child may be calmed by following the routine and completing the interrupted activity.

Prosocial Strategies

Social interaction is one of the most complex set of skills that a young child develops. It requires the integration of cognitive, language, and motor skills. An infant develops his or her first relationship with his or her parents or primary caregiver. This early attachment sets the pattern for future development of relationships and development of social skills. How a child behaves toward other people, how those people behave toward him or her, and the continuous interaction are indicators of social competence (i.e., the ability to achieve social goals successfully). It includes prosocial skills, such as caring for others, empathizing, helping, cooperating, and making friendships. You can enhance the development of these skills by modeling and using a curriculum that fosters these skills.

One of the most common reasons that parents want inclusion for their children is because they want them to be part of their neighborhood and to have friends. They want them to develop good social skills. Children with developmental delays often do not do well in group play and find it difficult to form reciprocal friendships. The place to develop such skills is in a real situation in which natural interactions with peers take place. Having peers who are good social models is an important factor. Physical proximity is a necessary but not sufficient factor for inclusion. You may have to employ specific strategies such as those listed below to foster social relationships and prosocial behavior in children.

1. Organize play sessions by grouping socially competent children with those who are less socially skilled.
2. Plan activities to help children develop alternative solutions to difficult social situations.
3. Assign an adult mediator to guide the conflict resolution.
4. Help children to learn to recognize that "help and cooperation" are appropriate in social situations. Point out and create helping situations for the children.

5. Help children to observe a play group they wish to enter, figure out the group's theme and purpose, and help them think of a role they could play or something they could contribute to the group. Teach children how to ask to be part of a group and how to join or be included in the play.
6. Help facilitate conversations that contribute to the maintenance of cohesive play.
7. Help children recognize, read, and respond to others' emotional cues.
8. Help the peer groups to understand a disliked child's behavior, but do not force peers to play with that child.
9. Suggest ways for the family to supplement and support the child's social acceptance, such as having a friend over after school.

◄○► ◄○► ◄○►

Francie, a teacher of 4-year-olds, learned that helping children get along and learn to cooperate may take many tries. Joseph watched intently while Charlie and Andre played with the dinosaurs, making caves and a jungle and dinosaur noises. Joseph then went and stood in the middle of the jungle. The boys started yelling and pushing him, "Get out of the way. You're messing up our game." Joseph started kicking the dinosaurs and the other boys yelled for Francie. Francie asked, "What do you think Joseph was doing when he stood in the middle?" Charlie said, "He's trying to bust in on our game. We don't want him. He can't talk." Francie said, "You are right, Joseph isn't talking yet, but I know he can make dinosaur noises. Show them, Joseph." Joseph obliged by making a loud growl. Francie said, "I know that there is a sharing rule in our classroom and that we have lots of dinosaurs. Please share them with Joseph." Francie took Joseph aside. "Joseph, here are some dinosaurs for you. Let's make a jungle next to the boys. When you want to play with them, what can you do?" Joseph signed, "Play?" Francie said, "That's right. You need to ask to play, not kick the toys." Joseph made his own jungle next to the boys. Andre noticed it. "Wow, Joseph, that's cool. Let's make a road between the two jungles. We can see if the tyrannosaurus can outrun the raptasaurus."

◄○► ◄○► ◄○►

Social relationships need to be helped to grow and flourish.

Successfully including a child with disabilities in a program is a complicated process. It requires thought and careful planning. Gathering important information about the child; making changes in the physical environment, equipment, and materials; adapting the schedule and the curriculum; and fostering new social relationships are all part of a successful process.

12

Staying Healthy

Janeen McCracken Taylor

◄○► ◄○► ◄○►

Jane, a child care worker, seemed to catch every cold and flu bug that visited her center. The children in her group appeared to have runny noses and chapped cheeks throughout the winter. Jane was tired of wiping noses. What could she do to regain her health and help her young students stay well?

◄○► ◄○► ◄○►

Catching colds or other minor illnesses is a common experience for young children and early childhood personnel. There are ways you can minimize the spread of disease among children, staff, and families in your program. The guidelines offered in this chapter are designed to help you and the children with whom you work stay as healthy as possible. In this chapter, you will learn to minimize disease transmission by learning about the following:

1. Procedures for

    -   Washing hands
    -   Cleaning up after a child who is ill or has an accident
    -   Diapering
    -   Wearing smocks
    -   Handling food properly

2. Guidelines for promoting health in child care settings

    In your career as an early childhood professional, you will have many decisions to make. Among the most important decisions will be those related to your health and the health of the children in your care. Increasing your understanding of how and why illness is spread and what you can do to minimize the risk of illness will be essential to good health for you, your young students, and families of the children in your program. This will be especially important

171

for children with disabilities, some of whom may be more vulnerable than their peers who do not have disabilities.

WHY DO YOUNG CHILDREN SEEM TO GET SICK SO OFTEN?

At the simplest level, germs (i.e., disease-carrying particles or microorganisms) cause most illnesses. Germs exist almost everywhere. If you carried a high-powered microscope with you and knew how to use it properly, you would be able to find germs in your home, at your workplace, in schools, at the mall, on all parts of your body, and even in your doctor's office. Early childhood settings are particularly good locations for germs to pass from one person to another because of a number of factors. Young children have not yet developed immunity to an arsenal of common illnesses and tend to get more colds, also known as upper respiratory infections (URIs), per year than adults (Crosson et al., 1986; Thacker, Addiss, Goodman, Holloway, & Spencer, 1992). Little ones also tend to play close to one another, share toys, or share food. These behaviors provide more opportunities for germs to pass from one child to another. Infants, toddlers, and some older children lack bowel or bladder control and need diapering or have toileting accidents. Because germs can be spread through contact with body fluids (e.g., urine), diaper changing and cleanup after toileting accidents can be times when children and adults are at greater risk of acquiring an illness.

Another way in which children might exchange germs is poor personal hygiene. If a child does not wash his or her hands after toileting and then touches objects or people, illness can be spread.

Car pools to and from child care centers or preschools are part of life for many working parents who juggle busy schedules. Children from two or more families are in proximity to one another during sometimes lengthy car rides and it would be nearly impossible for parents to keep children far enough apart from one another to keep sneezes and coughs from spreading germs.

HOW CAN YOU TELL WHEN A CHILD IS ILL?

Some illnesses have no symptoms or very mild symptoms. Others are contagious after infection but before symptoms are apparent. This is known as the incubation period. How many times do you hear parents say, "She was just so quiet. I knew she was coming down with something"? During incubation a child may be lethargic, stop eating, slow down, or act irritable.

> Although these symptoms do not necessarily warrant exclusion from the child care facility, close observation for further developing illness is indicated . . . symptoms such as diarrhea, vomiting, rash, skin lesions, wound infections, cough, or runny nose should alert personnel to the strong likelihood of infectious disease . . . and whenever possible another care source for these children should be sought. (Yamauchi, 1993, p. 10)

Common signs and symptoms of childhood infection are listed in Table 1.

Exclusion is not necessary for all of the signs and symptoms listed in Table 1; however, infants cared for in groups are prone to more infections than infants cared for at home. Yamauchi (1993) suggests excluding infants from group settings if they have any of the following signs and symptoms:

- Fever
- Rash accompanied by a fever
- Diarrhea (loose stool that cannot be contained with a diaper)
- Vomiting
- Unusual tiredness
- Poor feeding
- Persistent crying or irritability
- Breathing difficulties or persistent coughing
- Jaundice

DO CHILDREN WITH DISABILITIES GET
SICK MORE OFTEN THAN OTHER CHILDREN?

In general, children with disabilities pose no greater risk for infectious disease transmission than children who have no disabilities (Dilks, 1993). Children with certain disabling conditions may have greater susceptibility to specific kinds of illnesses, but most of the

Table 1.   Common signs and symptoms of childhood infection

Signs/symptoms	Possible illness
Coughing	Respiratory infection, sinusitis, pneumonia, influenza, pertussis, *Haemophilus influenzae,* and others
Diarrhea	Salmonella, Shigella, parasites, and others
Fever	May be a general symptom of viral or bacterial infection
Headache/stiff neck	May be a symptom of many illnesses, but with fever may represent bacterial or viral meningitis
Infected skin/sores	May be impetigo or wound infection; child should not be allowed in center without physician consent
Irritability/prolonged crying	May be a symptom of any illness, but with fever may represent bacterial or viral meningitis
Itching of body or scalp	Scabies or other lesions or agents
Lethargy	May be a general symptom of viral or bacterial disease
Pink eye	Tearing, itching, swelling, tenderness, and redness of the eye represents conjunctivitis, either viral or bacterial in nature
Rapid or altered breathing	Respiratory infections, as above
Rash	Must be evaluated on a case-by-case basis; whenever there is a question of cause, consult a physician
Sore throat	Respiratory infections, tonsillitis, viruses, strep throat
Vomiting	May be a general symptom of viral or bacterial diseases
Yellow skin or eyes	May be a symptom of hepatitis; child should not be allowed in child care without physician consent

Adapted from Yamauchi, T. (1993). Guidelines for attendees and personnel. In L.G. Donowitz (Ed.), *Infection control in the child care center and preschool* (2nd ed., p. 11). Baltimore: Williams & Wilkins; adapted by permission.

diseases of concern for children with disabilities cannot be transmitted easily. For example, children with spinal problems known as spina bifida are prone to urinary tract infections (UTIs), but UTIs are not spread easily between individuals (Andersen, Bale, Blackman, & Murph, 1986). Children with oral-motor problems are prone to respiratory infections caused by aspiration (i.e., coughing or choking while eating or drinking, causing food to go into the lungs; this can lead to a serious infection) of food during meals. Most illnesses affecting children with disabilities are a greater problem for the child with a disability than for peers without disabilities. In other words, a child without disabilities can pose a greater threat to the child with disabilities than the child with disabilities poses for the child without disabilities. Dilks (1993) suggests that children with disabilities should be subject to the same health considerations as children without disabilities.

Which Disabling Conditions Place Children at Greater Risk of Illness?

There are a number of disabling conditions that may cause a child to be at greater risk than usual for acquiring a communicable disease. Among the most common are cerebral palsy (CP), Down syndrome, pediatric acquired immunodeficiency syndrome (AIDS), and spina bifida.

Children with Cerebral Palsy   For children with CP, muscles controlling breathing, coughing, sneezing, and swallowing may be weak (Batshaw & Perret, 1992). This can lead to aspiration of food and subsequent pneumonia. Unproductive coughing from weak respiratory muscles allows mucus to build up in the respiratory tract and provides an ideal site for incubation of disease-causing germs. It is important to consult with the primary care provider for a child with CP to find out if you should watch for such signs of an impending infection as rapid or altered (e.g., shallow) breathing, fever, running nose, or sneezing (Yamauchi, 1993). Call the child's physician if there are any indications of infection or questions regarding the child's health (Dilks, 1993).

Children with Down Syndrome   Because of a number of factors, children with Down syndrome are prone to URIs and other communicable diseases. With low muscle tone and a range of potential congenital problems (e.g., abnormalities of the digestive tract or heart), a minor infection can engender greater health problems. Aggressive preventive measures are a good idea. Frequent hand washing and proper diapering techniques are especially important to minimize the risk of infection for children with Down syndrome. It is also important to monitor children with Down syndrome for listlessness, high temperature, rapid breathing, or increased pulse rates. "Such symptoms indicate the need for further medical evaluation" (Urbano, 1992, p. 31).

Children with AIDS   For children with pediatric AIDS there is always concern about the health of the affected child as well as the risk of infection for other children and adults. Batshaw and Perret (1992) report that "no cases of person-to-person transmission in day care centers or schools have been documented; the risk there is thought to be negligible" (p. 124). Children with AIDS have a limited ability to fight infection and are at greater risk of becoming ill from germs found in a group setting. Risks can be somewhat minimized by keeping the child at home during outbreaks of illness (e.g., colds, flu), but "most experts agree that the benefits of social contact outweigh the risk of infection, and that from a quality-of-life perspective, children should remain in school as much as possible" (p. 125).

Children with Spina Bifida "Spina bifida means cleft spine. It is an incomplete closure of the spinal column. It can involve the skin, spinal column, and spinal cord" (Urbano, 1992, p. 50). Because the nerves associated with bladder control may be affected by spina bifida, a child may require periodic insertion of a drainage tube into the urinary opening to empty the bladder. This procedure is known as clean intermittent catheterization. If the bladder is not emptied completely, the residual urine can predispose a child to bladder or kidney infections. Although this is not a problem for peers of the child with spina bifida, it is important for caregivers to know the signs and symptoms of infection in order to notify the child's family or health care provider of changes in the child's health status (Urbano, 1992). Be sure to check with the physician of a child with spina bifida for information about specific indications of illness.

ARE THERE ILLNESSES OF PARTICULAR CONCERN?

Although coughs, colds, and flu are annoying and can be temporarily debilitating, they are seldom a major health problem. There are, however, some illnesses of particular concern in child care settings (Aronson & Osterholm, 1984). First, children in group care are at greater risk of acquiring certain diseases primarily affecting younger children. *Haemophilus influenzae* (HiB) is an example of an illness that affects young children more frequently than adults. Fortunately, a vaccine, *Haemophilus influenzae* vaccine (HBVC), can decrease the likelihood of contracting this illness and can be given to children as young as 2 months of age (Shelov & Hannemann, 1991).

Second, some communicable diseases can affect both children and adults (i.e., staff, family members) and cause considerable discomfort. An example of this kind of illness is viral diarrhea that may be associated with painful abdominal cramps and dehydration.

Third, there are infections that cause few symptoms in young children, but can cause serious illness in adult staff or family contacts. Hepatitis A is often associated with mild fever, nausea, vomiting, diarrhea, or jaundice (i.e., a yellowish skin color) in children, however, "adults who contract this illness usually experience these problems to a much greater degree" (Shelov & Hannemann, 1991, p. 437). And last, there are communicable diseases with few, if any, health effects for children or adults, but are potentially harmful to an unborn child (Blackman, 1989; Pueschel & Mulick, 1990). Infections known to cause fetal damage (Williamson & Demmler, 1992) include rubella (i.e., German measles), cytomegalovirus (CMV), herpes simplex virus, human immunodeficiency virus (HIV) (Bale, 1990), and toxoplasmosis (i.e., a disease transmitted through contact with cat feces or improperly cooked meat). Because most child care workers are women of childbearing age, **it is critical to seek good prenatal care and follow all guidelines for minimizing the spread of disease.**

If you are pregnant or thinking of becoming pregnant, be sure to consult with an obstetrician. You should inform your doctor that you work with young children. Your doctor may order special blood tests to see if you have immunity to a number of diseases that can affect an unborn child and offer specific advice on how to stay healthy throughout a pregnancy. It is highly likely that your doctor will say the most important way to minimize illness is frequent and thorough hand washing (Finney, Miller, & Adler, 1993).

ACCURATE INFORMATION CAN MINIMIZE INFECTION TRANSMISSION

You should know how diseases are transmitted. If you need more information about the ways in which diseases are spread, ask your center director or officials from your local or state health agency to provide in-service education or printed materials related to infectious disease. Most illnesses affecting children are spread by 1) germs contained in tiny droplets exhaled by an infected person onto another person (or object) during breathing, sneezing, coughing, or spitting; 2) direct contact with a person who is ill; 3) direct contact with a contaminated object; 4) poor hygiene after toileting with subsequent hand to mouth touching; 5) contact with an infected person's body fluids; or 6) germs passing from mother to fetus during pregnancy (Taylor & Taylor, 1994). Some diseases can be transmitted in more than one way. For instance, cytomegalovirus can be transmitted by direct contact, oral–fecal contact, or respiratory droplets. The ways in which people can become infected with a communicable disease are known as *routes of transmission* and are summarized in Table 2.

Hand Washing Can Minimize Infection Transmission

The single most important behavior associated with lowering the risk of catching or transmitting an infectious disease is hand washing (Committee on Infectious Diseases, American Academy of Pediatrics, 1987). Hand washing should become routine throughout the day, especially at times indicated in Figure 1. To remind children and staff to wash their hands often and carefully, posters containing directions for thorough hand washing should be displayed prominently near every sink.

Table 2.   Common routes of transmission for communicable diseases

Germs exit from	Route of transmission	Germs enter through	Example illness
Respiratory tract	Aerosol	Mouth or nose	Influenza
Skin	Direct contact with infected person	Skin	Herpes simplex virus
Object	Direct contact with a contaminated object	Skin, mouth, nose, or other opening in the body	Upper respiratory infection (URI)
Intestinal tract	Oral–fecal	Mouth	Hepatitis A
Blood, urine, saliva, and so forth	Body fluids	Skin puncture	Hepatitis B
Mother's blood	Placental	Fetal blood	Acquired immunodeficiency syndrome

To wash your hands properly (Figure 2), use liquid soap, lots of running water, and plenty of brisk hand rubbing to scrub all surfaces of your hands and lower arms for a minimum of 10 seconds. You might try scrubbing for the time it takes to sing such simple songs as "Yankee Doodle" or "Pop Goes the Weasel." This will ensure enough time for a thorough cleaning of your hands and model a desirable behavior for children in your care. After rinsing with running water, use paper towels to dry your hands. Cloth towels and bar soaps are less desirable because they can harbor germs. Sinks equipped with knee or foot pedals are preferable to hand-operated faucets to avoid contamination from handles. If knee or foot pedals are not feasible, you can turn off faucets using paper towels as a barrier. For additional protection, spray faucet handles with disinfectant after each use, but make sure the disinfectant is stored out of children's reach. When you wash your hands properly and as frequently as recommended, you may develop dry, cracked, and chapped hands. Liberal use of skin creams and lotions can minimize skin problems. Good hygiene can reduce your risk of getting sick in a child care setting. Good hygiene also reduces the risk of illness in children.

Wash Your Hands Often, Especially
- Upon arrival at center
- Prior to eating or drinking
- After toileting
- After diaper changing
- After contact with an ill child
- After contact with infected items (e.g., tissues, mouthed toys, eating utensils)
- Before departure from center

Figure 1.   Appropriate times for hand washing. (Adapted from Taylor, J.M., & Taylor, W.S. [1994]. *Healthy child care.* In C.A. Baglin & M. Bender [Eds.], *Handbook on quality child care for young children: Settings, standards, and resources.* San Diego, CA: Singular; reprinted by permission.)

Step 1:	Turn on water and wet your hands thoroughly.
Step 2:	Use liquid soap to lather hands briskly for at least 10 seconds.
Step 3:	Rub hands briskly under running water until all soap has been removed.
Step 4:	Dry hands on paper towels.
Step 5:	If sink doesn't have knee- or pedal-operated faucets, use a paper towel to turn off water.
Step 6:	Use the paper towel to open the door to the bathroom.
Step 7:	Discard the paper towel in a lined trash can using a foot-operated lid.
Step 8:	Make sure the trash can has a tight cover and is out of children's reach.
Step 9:	Use hand lotion to keep skin from becoming dry.

Figure 2.   Proper hand-washing technique.

Clean Up Body Fluid Spills Safely

It is not uncommon for a healthy young child to have a bloody nose, occasional small cut, or skinned elbow. Children also may spit, drool, vomit, or have toileting accidents. Because some germs are spread through body fluids, you should clean up blood, vomit, saliva, mucus, urine, or feces immediately following any accident. As with diapering, consider using universal precautions for cleanup of body fluids. Keep an emergency cleanup kit in your classroom or home containing several pairs of latex gloves, paper towels, disinfectant, and plastic bags.

When a child is injured or becomes ill, first comfort the child. You can teach older children to use their hands to cover a scrape or cut and let you know about it right away. Next, get the emergency cleanup kit. For the cleanup, it is best to use what are known as "universal precautions." Universal precautions are measures taken when there may be contact with body fluids (Centers for Disease Control, 1987). "Practically, this means that gloves should be worn whenever contact with blood or blood-contaminated fluids is possible" (Urbano, 1992, p. 172). The American Academy of Pediatrics (1991) suggests using universal precautions when there is a high risk of spreading infection through direct contact or high-risk caregiving procedures. Because there are illnesses for which there are no apparent symptoms during the incubation period and others in which "shedding" (i.e., a way in which germs may be carried from the body via urine, feces, tears, and perspiration) occurs, it makes sense to be cautious with all children.

Use universal precautions when cleaning up a spill of body fluid (see Figure 3). Guidelines for universal precautions include 1) wearing a new pair of disposable gloves for each incident or child; 2) blotting the spill with paper towels to reduce the amount of liquid or contaminated material; 3) disposing of all contaminated material (e.g., soiled paper towels) in a doubled plastic bag that is clearly marked "Caution: contaminated materials"; 4) removing gloves and disposing of them in the same bag; 5) sealing and disposing of the bag (check with the local health department regarding disposal regulations); 6) putting on new gloves to clean the spill area

Step 1:	Wear gloves.	
Step 2:	Wipe up spill with paper towels.	
Step 3:	Place soiled paper towels and gloves in a doubled plastic bag and seal the bag.	
Step 4:	Put on fresh gloves.	
Step 5:	Wash area with soap or detergent and water.	
Step 6:	Rinse area with clean water.	
Step 7:	Disinfect area.	
Step 8:	Let area air dry.	
Step 9:	Dispose of all refuse outside children's areas.	
Step 10:	Store cleaning or disinfecting products out of child's reach.	

Figure 3. Guidelines for cleaning spills of body fluids. (Adapted from Taylor, J.M., & Taylor, W.S. [1989]. *Communicable disease and young children in group settings.* Austin, TX: PRO-ED; reprinted by permission.)

with a solution containing 1 part household bleach to 10 parts water (this must be made fresh daily); 7) putting on a new pair of gloves to clean remaining fluids; and 8) carefully removing the gloves for disposal. Latex gloves provide a barrier to germs and prevent contamination through direct contact with infectious material. Taylor and Taylor (1994) suggest additional steps for cleaning spills of body fluids:

> [A] concentration of bleach should be available in a pump spray bottle for application to small or hard-to-reach surfaces. Washed surfaces can be left to air dry, or after 20 minutes can be rinsed with clean water and then left to air dry. Disinfection should follow all spills of body fluids. **Bottles and storage containers of disinfectant, bleach, or bleach solutions should be clearly labeled and sealed with child resistant caps and kept out of a child's reach.** (p. 96)

Use Proper Diapering and Toileting Techniques

Because diaper changing can involve contact with feces or urine, both of which can contain infectious matter, it carries the risk of causing contamination for the child, caregiver, or environment (Child Day Care Infectious Disease Study Group, 1984). Gloves should be used for diaper changing, cleanup procedures, and toileting assistance (Finney et al., 1993). Clean gloves should be used for each child and diaper changing should be confined to designated areas separate from food preparation and serving areas.

Diaper-changing areas or tables should have washable surfaces and be located near a sink. A new disposable covering for the changing table should be placed under each child and discarded after one use. Contaminated disposable diapers and wipes should be placed in sealed plastic bags for disposal. Soiled diapers should be placed in plastic bags and discarded in a plastic-lined trash container with a foot pedal–operated lid. Trash cans should have tightly fitted lids and be kept out of the reach of children (e.g., outside the door or on a tall shelf). Soiled clothing also should be placed in plastic bags, sealed, and stored in a covered container until pick up by the parents. The changing surface should be washed and disinfected after every procedure. Finally, before returning to other activities, you and the child, as appropriate, should wash your hands carefully, even if you wear gloves during diaper changing.

Wear a Clean Smock Each Day

Almost any kind of clean cloth serves as an effective barrier against germs. Having clean smocks available makes good sense (Taylor & Taylor, 1989). If you put on a clean smock before the first child arrives each day, you may reduce your risk of becoming infected. Toss the smock into a plastic laundry bag before you leave work or when the last child departs, and launder the smocks in soapy hot water before the next use. Any kind of garment that covers most of your clothing provides a barrier against most germs. Such garments as men's shirts or oversized blouses are adequate for this purpose. An additional benefit of smocks is the protection they offer from messy materials (e.g., paint, glue, papier mâché).

Handle Food with Care

Ask a representative of the local public health agency for suggestions of individuals or organizations who can review your food handling practices and equipment (Committee on Early Childhood, Adoption and Dependent Care, American Academy of Pediatrics, 1987). Even if you are not required to have a review of this nature, it is important to ensure that you have healthful methods of preparing food, storing food, refrigerating perishables, and cleaning up after meals or snacks. Be especially careful of the ways you store infant formula and commercial baby foods. Yamauchi (1993) recommends discarding unused baby food or formula after 24 hours. Wash your hands before handling food and before feeding children. If you work in a large center, food preparation and service personnel should have no skin lesions or child care responsibilities.

IS THERE ANYTHING YOU CAN DO TO THE ENVIRONMENT TO PROMOTE GOOD HEALTH?

Most infectious disease protection measures could be classified as common sense. To minimize the risk of transmitting communicable diseases in child care settings, wash all play surfaces, toys, and walls with disinfectant each day. One part chlorine bleach diluted in 10 parts of water is an inexpensive disinfectant when used on washable surfaces. Use of carpeting is not advisable in a child care setting because carpeting is virtually impossible to disinfect or clean adequately. Floor tiles or other washable flooring is preferable to carpeting and should be swept and mopped with a disinfectant each day. Throw rugs that are machine washable should be acceptable if washed regularly. Collect trash in plastic bags, seal each bag, and dispose of the garbage in an appropriate manner daily.

Next, make sure you know how to minimize transmission of illness through environmental modifications. As suggested previously, food preparation should be carried out in areas that are separate from diaper-changing areas and each should have designated hand-washing facilities. For rest or nap times, cribs should be at least 3 feet apart to "decrease transmission of airborne pathogens, and bedding and mattresses should not be shared unless thoroughly cleaned first" (Yamauchi, 1993, p. 10). If you work in a child care center, you can get information on other environmental issues related to health from the **National Association for the Education of Young Children,** the **American Public Health Association,** and the **American Academy of Pediatrics.** These organizations offer suggestions regarding ventilation, temperature control, amount of space per child, number of lavatories per child, lay out of food preparation facilities, class size, and amount of outdoor play area (see Resources section at the end of this book). Research conducted in child care facilities indicates that appropriate hand washing, appropriate age groupings for children, and use of easily cleaned surfaces reduce the incidence of communicable diseases in child care centers (Petersen & Bressler, 1986).

In general, health care experts suggest isolating ill children. Children who become ill while at a care center should be kept apart from children who are not ill. Even though it is likely that germs responsible for an illness contracted by a child at a center already have been spread to several other people before symptoms appear, it makes good sense to separate ill children until they have been picked up by their parents or a medical evaluation has been performed (Taylor & Taylor, 1994).

WHERE CAN YOU GET ADDITIONAL INFORMATION?

Your local and state public health care agencies can provide additional information regarding minimizing disease transmission and other aspects of healthy child care. Find out which diseases are potential community health problems and obtain lists of diseases that can affect large groups and must be reported to the health department. Reportable diseases usually are grouped into three categories 1) diseases that can have considerable impact on public health and should be reported immediately (e.g., tuberculosis); 2) common diseases that have a substantial public health impact but do not require urgent reporting (e.g., hepatitis A); and 3) routine infections for which reporting is requested only during outbreaks (e.g., measles). Gather information about these kinds of diseases, become familiar with their signs and symptoms, and report any occurrences to the proper authorities (Taylor & Taylor, 1994).

HOW CAN YOU PROMOTE GOOD HEALTH?

Your health is extremely important to minimizing the spread of communicable diseases. If you work at a center, pre-employment medical evaluations, which specifically address health issues related to child care, are extremely important. If your center does not require a medical evaluation, urge the director to institute a policy of this nature. If you care for children in your home, be sure to have regular physical examinations by your primary health care provider. At a minimum, health examinations should include 1) a history of infectious diseases; 2) a review of immunizations; 3) immunization, if appropriate; 4) a physical examination; and 5) antibody testing for exposure to specific diseases (e.g., for measles, German measles, mumps, herpes simplex virus, CMV, hepatitis, HIV). Child care administrators should be aware that any information obtained from a physician or other health practitioner as the result of a medical evaluation is confidential and may not be released unless the employee has given written permission. Health evaluation findings should remain confidential when transferred to an employee's file.

KEEP CURRENT ON HEALTH ISSUES AFFECTING CHILD CARE

Well-trained child care providers offer higher quality child care and a lower risk of communicable diseases (Berk, 1985; Stallings & Porter, 1980). Be sure to read and attend seminars that offer updates on communicable disease transmission, prevention, recognition of illness in children, behavior management, nutrition, caregiving for children with chronic health conditions, cardiopulmonary resuscitation, and first aid procedures.

Parent education related to health is very important. When families enroll their child in your program, parents should be provided with written materials containing your policies regarding communicable diseases and parents' responsibility regarding notification of the center if their child is ill. Due to the frequency of illness in young children, communicable disease transmission is inevitable, but parents should be reminded that group care can increase a child's incidence of illness (Adler, 1988). Written updates (e.g., a short newsletter) to families of children in your care can offer information regarding each family's responsibility for informing you or your director when a child has signs or symptoms of illness.

Consider the Services of a Health Care Consultant

Due to the frequency of illness in group settings for young children, and the importance of rapid recognition and management of infectious diseases, you might want to ask a pediatrician, pediatric nurse practitioner, family nurse practitioner, family practitioner with pediatric experience, or public health nurse to provide consultative services to you or to your program. In general, health care consultants would not offer diagnostic or treatment services for ill children, but would provide communicable disease oversight. They can review child health records for evidence of annual physical examinations by physicians, health problems that might affect others, health issues warranting special attention (e.g., dietary restrictions), or evidence of current immunizations.

Health consultants can monitor occurrences of communicable diseases and, in the event of a communicable disease, could gather and interpret relevant medical information. For example, if one or more of the children in your care develops hepatitis A, the health consultant could expedite notification of local public health officials, administer immune globulin to contacts of the infected child, notify families, notify other children's physicians, and implement other health measures necessary to control the outbreak.

Ask for Administrative Guidance

Every child care program should have a written policy manual with policies related to child and health care procedures. State and local health regulations pertaining to child care, guidelines for obtaining health consultation, sick child care, staff illness, procedures for disinfecting rooms or materials, and exclusion of ill children or adults should be clearly delineated. Also, policies should be included for contacting families of children who return to child care centers following an illness. Information regarding the likelihood of recurrence, route of transmission, and special precautions to minimize potential transmission should be sought. This can be facilitated through good communication with families, primary health care providers, and public health officials.

Contrary to popular belief, there appears to be no evidence that children prolong their recovery by attending school while mildly ill if staffing is adequate. Many communicable diseases are transmitted before symptoms appear. Therefore, some exclusion policies may not be effective in preventing contagion. If mildly ill children can be cared for without compromising the health and care of others, exclusion may not be warranted according to Shapiro, Kuritsky, and Potter (1986). To minimize confusion for families, a sick child care policy and exclusion policy should be clearly written and distributed to parents on their first visit.

Know the Child Care Regulations in Your State

Most states have regulations, albeit varied, for the following health practices:

- Hand washing
- Employee health examinations
- Use of personal toilet articles
- Medical record keeping
- Health-related admission procedures
- Isolation of ill children or adults
- Return to care after illness
- Notification of parents concerning outbreaks of communicable diseases
- Reportable diseases

- Adult–child ratios
- Group size (Morgan, Stevenson, Fiene, & Stephens, 1986)

It is important for administrators to become knowledgeable about regulatory requirements in their state and ensure that all staff comply with regulations affecting child, family, and staff health.

MAINTAIN CONFIDENTIALITY AT ALL TIMES

In a small child care program, it may be hard to respect a child's or family's confidentiality, but many states have clear regulatory requirements regarding confidentiality. If a child has a communicable disease (e.g., hepatitis A), a center's staff is expected to hold that child's identity in confidence. However, there is also an obligation to provide a safe and healthful environment for all children attending the program. Know the regulations regarding confidentiality in your state and develop policies that are in accord with regulatory parameters.

Even vigilant efforts will not prevent all illness. If an outbreak occurs, parents should be notified promptly while maintaining the confidentiality of the infected child. It is imperative that other families receive information regarding the possibility of infection. To avoid a breach of confidentiality, a general letter containing a description of the illness should be sent to all families of children enrolled at the program. Information about the illness, its characteristics, the ways it is transmitted, likelihood of infection, and precautionary or treatment measures should be included in the letter. If informative materials are prepared prior to an outbreak, they can be distributed in a timely fashion without violating confidentiality. Excellent examples of letters to parents (see Figure 4) and informa-

---

Date:

Dear Parent or caretaker:

A child (or adult) from our center has contracted Hepatitis A.

WHAT IS IT? Hepatitis A is an infection of the liver and may cause fatigue, elevated body temperature, poor appetite, nausea, or jaundice (yellowing of skin or eyes). Hepatitis A usually lasts for a week or two. Young children may have very mild symptoms or none at all.

HOW IS IT CAUGHT? Hepatitis A is caused by germs in the intestines and stool. Hepatitis A germs are passed in stool. If an infected person does not wash hands thoroughly after toileting, the virus can spread to other people, food, or objects. Two to eight weeks after being infected, a person may develop Hepatitis A. This illness is diagnosed by a blood test. Hepatitis A may be prevented by a shot of immune globulin.

WHAT SHOULD BE DONE?

1. Make sure everyone washes their hands thoroughly after using the toilet, helping a child use the toilet, changing a diaper, cleaning up toilet accidents, and before touching food (or eating).
2. If anyone in your home develops symptoms, have them see a physician right away and tell your health care provider about this letter.
3. Ask your health care provider or a local health department official if you or other family members should have a shot of immune globulin.

If you have any questions, please contact your health care provider or the local health department.

Figure 4.   Example of a letter to parents regarding a child with an illness. (From Taylor, J.M., & Taylor, W.S. [1994]. Healthy child care. In C.A. Baglin & M. Bender [Eds.], *Handbook on quality child care for young children: Settings, standards, and resources*. San Diego, CA: Singular; reprinted by permission.)

tion sheets can be found in *Health in Day Care: A Manual for Day Care Providers* (Georgetown University Child Development Center, 1986).

SUMMARY

There is no way to eliminate all infectious disease from child care programs. There are precautions and guidelines designed to decrease the number of communicable diseases for young children and their adult caregivers. Such policies and practices as universal precautions for cleaning up after a child is ill or has an accident, proper diapering techniques, wearing smocks, and handling food properly will support good health and be effective in preventing or minimizing the transmission of diseases. Your ongoing education and the education of parents whose children are in your care are important issues to consider in promoting good health.

References

Abraham, M., Morris, L., & Wald, P. (1993). *The inclusive classroom*. Tuscon, AZ: Communication Skill Builders.

Adler, S.P. (1988). Molecular epidemiology of cytomegalovirus: Viral transmission among children attending a day care center, their parents, and caretakers. *Journal of Pediatrics, 112,* 366–372.

Alberto, P.A., & Troutman, A.C. (1982). *Applied behavior analysis for teachers*. Columbus, OH: Charles E. Merrill.

Americans with Disabilities Act and Head Start: Practical strategies for developing compliance plans. (1992–1993). *Great Lakes Regional Access Project Quarterly Resource, 7,* 1.

Americans with Disabilities Act of 1990 (ADA), PL 101-336. (July 26, 1990). Title 42, U.S.C. 12101 et seq: *U.S. Statutes at Large, 104,* 327–378.

Andersen, R.D., Bale, J.F., Blackman, J.A., & Murph, J.R. (1986). *Infections in children: A sourcebook for educators and child care providers*. Rockville, MD: Aspen Publishers, Inc.

Aronson, S.S., & Osterholm, M.T. (1984, December). Prevention and management of infectious diseases in child care. *Child Care Information Exchange*, pp. 8–10.

Bale, J.F. (1990). The neurologic complications of AIDS in infants and young children. *Infants and Young Children: An Interdisciplinary Journal of Special Child Care Practices, 3*(2), 15–23.

Batshaw, M.L., & Perret, Y.M. (1992). *Children with disabilities: A medical primer* (3rd ed.). Baltimore: Paul H. Brookes Publishing Co.

Berk, L. (1985). Relationship of educational attainment, child-oriented attitudes, job satisfaction, and career commitment to caregiver behavior toward children. *Child Care Quarterly, 14,* 103–129.

Blackman, J.A. (1989). *Medical aspects of developmental disabilities in children birth to three* (3rd ed.). Rockville, MD: Aspen Publishers, Inc.

Bredekamp, S. (1987). *Developmentally appropriate practice in early childhood programs serving children from birth through age 8*. Washington, DC: National Association for the Education of Young Children.

Centers for Disease Control. (1987). Update: Recommendations for prevention of HIV transmission in health-care settings. *Morbidity and Mortality Weekly Report, 36,* 1–18.

Child Care Law Center. (1993). *Caring for children with special needs: The Americans with Disabilities Act and child care*. San Francisco: Author.

Child Day Care Infectious Disease Study Group. (1984). Public health considerations of infectious diseases in child care centers. *Journal of Pediatrics, 105,* 1683–1686.

Children's Defense Fund. (1994). *The state of America's children yearbook*. Washington, DC: Author.

Committee on Early Childhood, Adoption and Dependent Care, American Academy of Pediatrics. (1987). *Health in day care: A manual for health professionals.* Elk Grove Village, IL: American Academy of Pediatrics.

Committee on Infectious Diseases, American Academy of Pediatrics. (1987). Health guidelines for the attendance in day-care and foster care settings of children infected with human immunodeficiency virus. *Pediatrics, 3,* 466–471.

Cronburg, J.G., Barnett, J., & Goldman, N. (1993). *Readily achievable checklist: A survey for accessibility.* Boston: Adaptive Environments Center.

Crosson, F.J., Black, S.B., Trumpp, C.E., Grossman, M., Lé, C.T., & Yeager, A.S. (1986). *Infections in day care centers: Current problems in pediatrics, 16*(3), 122–184.

DeHaas-Warner, S. (1994). The role of child care professionals in placement and programming decisions for preschoolers with special needs in community-based settings. *Young Children, 48*(5), 76–78.

Dilks, S. (1993). The child with disabilities. In L.G. Donowitz (Ed.), *Infection control in the child care center and preschool* (2nd ed., pp. 49–54). Baltimore: Williams & Wilkins.

Doggett, L., & George, J. (1993). *All kids count, child care and the Americans with Disabilities Act.* Arlington, TX: The Arc.

Education for All Handicapped Children Act of 1975, PL 94-142. (August 23, 1977). Title 20, U.S.C. 1401 et seq: *U.S. Statutes at Large, 89,* 773–796.

Education of the Handicapped Act Amendments of 1986, PL 99-457. (October 8, 1986). Title 20, U.S.C. 1400 et seq: *U.S. Statutes at Large, 100,* 1145–1177.

Finney, J.W., Miller, K.N., & Adler, S.P. (1993). Changing protective and risky behaviors to prevent child-to-parent transmission of cytomegalovirus. *Journal of Applied Behavior Analysis, 26,* 471–472.

Georgetown University Child Development Center. (1986). *Health in day care: A manual for day care providers.* Washington, DC: Author.

Goldberg, D., & Goldberg, M. (1993). *The Americans with Disabilities Act: A guide for people with disabilities, their families, and advocates.* Minneapolis, MN: The Pacer Center.

Goldman, N. (Ed.). (1991). *Achieving physical and communication accessibility.* Washington, DC: National Center for Access Unlimited.

Guralnick, M.J. (1990). Social competence and early intervention. *Journal of Early Intervention, 14*(1), 3–14.

Haring, N.G., & Schiefelbusch, R.L. (Eds.). (1976). *Teaching special children.* New York: McGraw-Hill.

Individuals with Disabilities Education Act of 1990 (IDEA), PL 101-476. (October 30, 1990). Title 20, U.S.C. 1400 et seq: *U.S. Statutes at Large, 104,* 1103–1151.

Kalscheur, J.A. (1992). Benefits of the Americans with Disabilities Act of 1990 for children and adolescents with disabilities. *The American Journal of Occupational Therapy, 46*(5), 419–426.

Koralek, D.G., Colker, L.J., & Dodge, D.T. (1993). *The what, why, and how of high-quality early childhood education: A guide for on-site supervision.* Washington, DC: National Association for the Education of Young Children.

Morgan, C.G., Stevenson, C.S., Fiene, R., & Stephens, K.O. (1986). Gaps and excesses in the regulation of child day care: Report of a panel. *Reviews of Infectious Diseases, 8,* 634–643.

Petersen, N.J., & Bressler, G.K. (1986). Design and modification of the day care center environment. *Reviews of Infectious Diseases, 8,* 618–621.

Pueschel, S.M., & Mulick, J.A. (1990). *Prevention of developmental disabilities.* Baltimore: Paul H. Brookes Publishing Co.

Rehabilitation Act of 1973, PL 93-112. (September 26, 1973). Title 29, U.S.C. 701 et seq: *U.S. Statutes at Large, 87,* 355–394.

Shapiro, E.D., Kuritsky, J., & Potter, J. (1986). Policies for the exclusion of ill children from group day care: An unresolved dilemma. *Reviews of Infectious Diseases, 8,* 622–625.

Shelov, S.P., & Hannemann, R.E. (Eds.). (1991). *Caring for your baby and your child: Birth to age 5.* New York: Bantam.

Stallings, J., & Porter, A. (1980). *National day care home study.* Palo Alto, CA: SRI International.

Taylor, J.M., & Taylor, W.S. (1989). *Communicable disease and young children in group settings.* Austin, TX: PRO-ED.

Taylor, J.M., & Taylor, W.S. (1994). Healthy child care. In C.A. Baglin & M. Bender (Eds.), *Handbook on quality child care for young children: Settings, standards, and resources* (pp. 87–106). San Diego, CA: Singular.

Thacker, S.B., Addiss, D.G., Goodman, R.A., Holloway, B.R., & Spencer, H.D. (1992). Infectious diseases and injuries in child day care: Opportunities for healthier children. *Journal of the American Medical Association, 268*(13), 1720–1796.

U.S. Equal Employment Opportunity Commission and the U.S. Department of Justice. (1991). *Americans with disabilities handbook.* Washington, DC: Author.

Urbano, M.T. (1992). *Preschool children with special health care needs.* San Diego, CA: Singular.

Williamson, W.D., & Demmler, G.J. (1992). Congenital infections: Clinical outcome and educational implications. *Infants and Young Children: An Interdisciplinary Journal of Special Care Practices, 4*(4), 1–10.

Wittmer, D.S., & Honig, A.S. (1994). Encouraging positive social development in young children. *Young Children, 49*(5), 4–19.

Yamauchi, T. (1993). Guidelines for attendees and personnel. In L.G. Donowitz (Ed.), *Infection control in the child care center and preschool* (2nd ed., pp. 9–22). Baltimore: Williams & Wilkins.

Glossary

Autism   A developmental disability that significantly affects verbal and nonverbal communication and social interaction and is generally evident before age 3. It is considered a neurological disorder. Other characteristics often associated with autism are engagement in repetitive activities and stereotyped movements, resistance to environmental change or change in daily routines, and unusual responses to sensory experiences.

Auxiliary aids and services   A range of services and devices for ensuring effective communication. They include qualified interpreters, notetakers, telephone handset amplifiers, assistive listening devices, open and closed captioning, telecommunication devices for deaf people (TDDs or TTYs), other effective methods of making aurally delivered materials available to individuals with hearing impairments, qualified readers, braille materials, large print materials, other effective methods of making visually delivered materials available to individuals with visual impairments, and acquisition or modification of equipment or devices.

Barrier free   Accessible to individuals with disabilities.

Child Find   The evaluation service provided by local school systems to assist in identifying young children; it begins the process of obtaining special education services.

Deaf-blindness   Concomitant hearing and visual impairments, the combination of which causes such severe communication and other developmental and educational problems that they cannot be accommodated in special education programs solely for children with blindness or deafness.

Deafness   A hearing impairment that is so severe that a child is unable to hear and understand spoken words, with or without amplification.

Developmental delay   A designation for children, usually ages birth to 5, who are experiencing delays, as defined by their state and measured by appropriate diagnostic instruments and procedures, in one or more of the following areas: physical development, cognitive development, communication development, social or emotional development, or adaptive development; and who therefore need education and related services. The extent of the delays may range from mild to severe.

Direct threat   A significant risk to the health or safety of others that cannot be eliminated by a modification of policies, practices, or procedures or by the provision of auxiliary aids or services.

Disinfectants   Chemical sanitizing agents, usually liquids, that inactivate or kill disease-causing particles (microorganisms).

Due process procedures   Those procedures that safeguard the rights of children with disabilities under IDEA.

Eligibility   A determination that a child fits into one of the disability categories under IDEA and may receive special education services.

Essential functions   Tasks that are fundamental and necessary to perform in a given employment position.

Germs   Microscopic particles (microorganisms) that can cause illness.

Hearing impairment   A hearing loss, whether permanent or fluctuating.

Inclusion   The philosophy that all children have the right to be included with their peers in all age-appropriate activities throughout life.

Individual with a disability   An individual with a physical or mental impairment that substantially limits one or more major life activities, has a record of such an impairment, or is regarded as having an impairment.

Incubation period   The time interval from the entrance of an organism into a person (host) until sickness is apparent.

Infect   The entrance of a disease-causing germ (microorganism) into or on a person's body.

Infectious diseases   Illnesses that can be transmitted; they also are known as *communicable*.

Integration   Specifically designed programs to combine typical children and children with disabilities.

Least restrictive environment   Terminology from IDEA that states that children with disabilities should be educated in an environment that is not more restrictive than their needs require.

Mainstreaming   Programs for children without disabilities in which some children with disabilities are enrolled.

Major life activities   Functions such as caring for oneself, performing manual tasks, walking, seeing, hearing, speaking, breathing, learning, and working.

Mental retardation Significantly below-average general intellectual functioning existing concurrently with limitations in adaptive behavior (the ability to meet the demands of the environment through age-appropriate, independent adaptive skills, communication, and play).

Multi-age grouping A group of children of more than one age who are combined for developmental programming.

Multiple disabilities Concomitant impairments such as mental retardation–blindness and mental retardation–orthopedic impairment, the combination of which causes such severe educational problems that they cannot be accommodated in a program solely for one of the impairments.

Orthopedic impairment Any condition that involves muscles, bones, or joints and is characterized by difficulty with movement. The term includes impairments caused by congenital anomaly (e.g., clubfoot, absence of a body limb), impairments caused by disease (e.g., poliomyelitis, bone tuberculosis), and impairments from other causes (e.g., cerebral palsy, amputations, fractures or burns that cause contractures). In educational or noneducational settings, orthopedic impairment affects the ability to perform small or large muscle activities or to perform adaptive skills.

Other health impairment A condition that limits strength, vitality, or alertness as a result of a chronic or acute health problem. Examples include cancer, some neurological disorders, rheumatic fever, severe asthma, uncontrolled seizure disorders, heart conditions, lead poisoning, diabetes, acquired immunodeficiency syndrome (AIDS), blood disorders (e.g., hemophilia, sickle cell anemia), cystic fibrosis, heart disease, and attention deficit disorder.

Public accommodation A facility, operated by a private entity, whose operations affect commerce and fall within at least one of the following categories: A nursery; private school or other place of education; child care center; or a private entity that owns, leases (or leases to), or operates a place of public accommodation.

Qualified individual with a disability An individual with a disability who, with or without reasonable accommodation, can perform the essential functions of the employment position that such an individual holds or desires.

Readily achievable Easily accomplishable and able to be carried out without much difficulty or expense.

Reasonable accommodations Changes in the job so that the job can be done by an individual with a disability.

Related services Transportation and other developmental, corrective, and support services required to assist a child with a disability to benefit from special education.

Occupational therapy   Services that help a child in fine motor, oral-motor, perceptual-motor, sensory processing, and activities of daily living.

Physical therapy   Services that help a child develop and use motor skills related to coordination, balance, muscle strength, endurance, range of motion, and mobility.

Speech-language therapy   Services that are provided by a speech-language pathologist who specializes in communication disorders such as voice quality, pronunciation (articulation), oral-motor skills, vocabulary (language), and hearing.

Religious entity   A religious entity controlled by a religious organization, including a place of worship.

Severe emotional disturbance   A disorder in which a child has behavioral or emotional responses that are extremely different from other children with the same ethnic or cultural background. These extreme behaviors impair social relationships and adaptive skills and are very disruptive in the classroom.

The term means a condition that includes the presence of one or more of the following characteristics over a long period of time and to a marked degree that adversely affects a child's educational performance:

1.   An inability to learn that cannot be explained by intellectual, sensory, or health factors
2.   An inability to build or maintain satisfactory interpersonal relationships with peers and teachers
3.   Inappropriate types of behavior or feelings under normal circumstances
4.   A general pervasive mood of unhappiness or depression
5.   A tendency to develop physical symptoms or fears associated with personal or school problems

The term includes schizophrenia. The term does not apply to children who are socially maladjusted, unless it is determined that they have a serious emotional disturbance.

Signs   Objective manifestations of a disease, such as fever, jaundice, or rash.

Special education   Specially designed instruction, provided at no cost to parents, which meets their child's unique needs.

Specific learning disability   A disorder in one or more of the basic psychological processes involved in understanding or using spoken or written language. Children may have difficulty listening, thinking, speaking, writing, spelling, and doing mathematical calculations. The term includes such conditions as perceptual disabilities, traumatic brain injury, minimal brain dysfunction, dyslexia, and developmental aphasia. The term does not apply to children who have learning problems that are primarily the result of visual, hearing, or motor disabilities; of mental retardation; of emotional disturbance; or of environmental, cultural, or economic disadvantage.

Speech and language impairments Communication disorders such as stuttering, impaired articulation, or voice impairment. This category also includes the inability to express oneself or an inability to understand what is being said.

Symptoms Subjective complaints of a person afflicted with a disease, such as pain or weakness.

Team teaching A method of developing a program for a child that uses information and combined efforts of all service providers.

Traumatic brain injury An injury to the brain caused by an external physical force, resulting in total or partial functional disability or psychosocial impairment or both. The term applies to open or closed head injuries resulting in impairments in one or more areas, such as cognition; language; memory; attention; reasoning; abstract thinking; judgment; problem solving; sensory, perceptual, and motor abilities; psychosocial behavior; physical functions; information processing; and speech. The term does not apply to brain injuries that are congenital or degenerative, or brain injuries induced by birth trauma.

Undue burden Significant difficulty or expense.

Undue hardship An action requiring significant difficulty or expense.

Visual impairment Any loss of sight that, with or without correction, adversely affects a child's learning. Blindness refers to a condition with no vision or only light perception. Low vision refers to limited distance vision or the ability to see only items close to the eyes.

Resources

This resources section includes those agencies, books, and articles that have helped us in preparing the material for this book. We also have included resources that child care providers have told us were helpful to them as they learned about inclusion, disabilities, and the laws.

The resources are grouped by chapter and categorized by written materials, videotapes, and agencies. The comments following each resource are descriptions from our experience and should not be considered a critical review.

PART I: HOW DO DISABILITY LAWS AFFECT YOUR CHILD CARE PROGRAM?

Chapter 1: The Americans with Disabilities Act: Child Care as a Public Accommodation

Written Materials

Child Care Law Center. (1993). *Caring for children with special needs: The Americans with Disabilities Act and child care.* San Francisco, CA: Author. (Available from Child Care Law Center, 22 Second Street, 5th Floor, San Francisco, CA 94105; [415] 495-5498). A concise, clear overview of how the ADA affects child care.

Doggett, L., & George, J. (1993). *All kids count: Child care and the Americans with Disabilities Act.* Arlington, TX: The Arc National Headquarters. (Available from The Arc, Post Office Box 1047, Arlington, TX 76004; [817] 261-6003, [817] 277-0553 [TDD]). Gives brief overview of Title III of the ADA and examples of how to include children with special needs and how to find resources. It includes an extensive resource list.

Horn, R.L. (1991). The education of children and youth with special needs: What do the laws say? *NICHY News Digest, 1*(1). (Available from National Information Center for Children and Youth with Disabilities, Post Office Box 1492, Washington, D.C. 20013; 1-800-

999-5599). This issue of the digest gives a succinct overview of laws pertaining to young children with disabilities. The publication is free and provides information on a variety of topics about disabilities. The organization provides fact sheets for each state with state disability agencies and resources.

Individuals with Disabilities Education Act Amendments of 1991, PL 102-119. (October 7, 1991). Title 20, U.S.C. 1400 et seq: *U.S. Statutes at Large, 105,* 587–608. To obtain a copy of IDEA you must get copies of the *Federal Register* for September 29, 1992 and October 27, 1992 from the following:

> Karen Edelen
> Office of Special Education Programs
> 3611 Switzer Building
> 400 Maryland Avenue, SW
> Washington, D.C. 20202
> (202) 205-8824
> or
> LRP Publications
> 747 Dresher Road
> Post Office Box 980
> Horsham, PA 19044-0980
> (215) 784-0860

Individuals with Disabilities Education Act Regulations. (1994). Title 34, *Code of Federal Regulations,* Part 300–399. (Available from Government Printing Office, Washington, D.C. 20402; [202] 783-3238). These regulations provide an expanded description of what must be provided under PL 94-142, the Education for All Handicapped Children Act and subsequent amendments.

U.S. Department of Justice, Civil Rights Division, Office on the Americans with Disabilities Act. (1992). *The Americans with Disabilities Act: Title III technical assistance manual.* Washington, DC: U.S. Government Printing Office. A detailed guide to the requirements of Title III, including examples.

Agencies

State Department of Education, Office of Special
Education Local School System, Division of Special Education

These agencies are given the responsibility under IDEA for ensuring and providing free, appropriate educational services to eligible children with disabilities.

State and Local Interagency
Coordinating Council for Part H Services

These agencies can provide information about services to infants and toddlers with disabilities.

U.S. Department of Education
Office of Civil Rights
600 Independence Avenue, SW
Washington, D.C. 20202
(202) 205-5439

This office can give you the telephone number for your regional office. It is responsible for investigating any Section 504 violations.

U.S. Department of Justice
Civil Rights Division
Coordination and Review
Post Office Box 66118
Washington, D.C. 20035-6118
(202) 514-0301 (voice)
(202) 514-0381 (TDD)

This agency is in charge of investigating violations of the ADA under Titles I and III.

Chapter 2: Employees in Child Care Settings Under the ADA

Written Materials

Child Care Law Center. (1993). *Caring for children with special needs: The Americans with Disabilities Act and child care.* San Francisco, CA: Author. (Available from Child Care Law Center, 22 Second Street, 5th Floor, San Francisco, CA 94105; [415] 495-5498). This book includes information about the ADA and the answers to some questions child care providers may be asking.

Doggett, L., & George, J. (1993). *All kids count: Child care and the Americans with Disabilities Act.* Arlington, TX: The Arc National Headquarters. (Available from The Arc, Post Office Box 1047, Arlington, TX 76004; [817] 261-6003 or [817] 277-0553 TDD). A very helpful guide about the ADA and serving children with special needs.

Meservey, L. (1993, July). Implications of the Americans with Disabilities Act. *Child Care Information Exchange, 92,* 81–83. A short article that summarizes how the employment provisions of the ADA affect child care centers.

U.S. Equal Employment Opportunity Commission. (1992, January). *A technical assistance manual on the employment provisions (Title I) of the Americans with Disabilities Act.* Washington, DC: Author.

U.S. Equal Employment Opportunity Commission and the U.S. Department of Justice. (1991). *Americans with disabilities handbook.* Washington, DC: Author. A definitive handbook that includes the law, the regulations, information about related laws, answers to many questions, and the Americans with Disabilities Act Accessibility Guidelines.

PART II: MAKING INCLUSION WORK IN YOUR PROGRAM: ADMINISTRATIVE ISSUES

Chapter 4: Addressing Staff Concerns

Written Materials

Division of Early Childhood of the Council for Exceptional Children and The National Association for the Education of Young Children (NAEYC). (1993). *Understanding the ADA*. Washington, DC: NAEYC. (Available from NAEYC, 1509 16th Street, NW, Washington, D.C. 20036-1426; 1-800-424-2460). This brochure gives a brief description of the ADA and a short list of resources.

Videotapes

Child and Family Services. (1991). *Just a kid like me* [Video]. (Available from Child and Family Services, 626 North Coronado Terrace, Los Angeles, CA 90026). This videotape shows the inclusion of different children into several child care settings.

Texas Planning Council for Developmental Disabilities. (1993). The ABC's of inclusive child care [Video]. (Available from Texas Planning Council for Developmental Disabilities, 4900 North Lamar Boulevard, Austin, TX 78751-2399; [512] 483-4080). A short videotape that is free of charge. It briefly explains inclusion of children with special needs into child care programs.

WETA. (1988). *Regular lives* [Video]. (Available from WETA, Post Office Box 2626, Washington, D.C. 20013; [703] 998-2600). This videotape discusses the philosophy of inclusion and shows children of various ages. Children, parents, and teachers talk about their experiences.

Chapter 5: Program Changes

Written Materials

Cronburg, J.G., Barnett, J., & Goldman, N. (1993). *Readily achievable checklist: A survey for accessibility*. Boston: Adaptive Environments Center. (Available from the American Occupational Therapy Association, 1383 Piccard Drive, Post Office Box 1725, Rockville, MD 20849-1725; [301] 948-9626, 1-800-377-8555 [TDD], or Adaptive Environments Center, 374 Congress Street, Suite 301, Boston, MA 02210; [617] 695-1225 [Voice/TDD]). This booklet contains a process to evaluate the accessibility of a facility.

The Great Lakes Resource Access Project. (1992–1993). *The Americans with Disabilities Act and Head Start: Practical strategies for developing compliance plans* [Quarterly Resource], *7*(1). (Available from Great Lakes Resource Access Project, University of Illinois, Department of Special Education, 403 East Healey, Champaign, IL 61820; [217] 333-3876).

Agencies

Architectural and Transportation
Barriers Compliance Board (Access Board)
1331 F Street, NW, S-1000
Washington, D.C. 20004-1111
1-800-USA-ABLE; 202-653-7835 (voice and TDD)

This agency can provide Americans with Disabilities Act Accessibility Guidelines (ADAAG) information and has information about accessibility in children's facilities in the future.

Technical Assistance Centers

The National Institute on Disability and Rehabilitation Research (NIDRR) has funded 10 regional centers for 5 years to provide information, training, and technical assistance related to implementation of the ADA. To be connected directly to the regional center serving your state, call 1-800-949-4232 (voice and TDD).

Telephone Company

Contact your local telephone company for the number of the state relay center. AT&T Telecommunication Relay Services and Operator Services for people who are deaf, deaf-blind, hard of hearing, or have a speech impairment can be contacted at the following numbers: 1-800-855-2880 (TT/TTY); 1-800-855-2881 (voice); 1-800-855-2882 (ASCII); and 1-800-855-2883 (Telebraille).

Chapter 7: Understanding Special Education Services

Agencies

The Council for Exceptional Children
1920 Association Drive
Reston, VA 22091-1589
1-800-845-6232 (voice and TTY)

A professional organization that provides information about all children with special needs. It includes a Division of Early Childhood.

National Information Center for Children
and Youth with Disabilities (NICHY)
Post Office Box 1492
Washington, D.C. 20013
1-800-999-5599

State and Local Education Agencies

These agencies offer extensive information about how the education for children with disabilities is provided in your state and community. In particular, ask for information for parents about Child-Find services, individualized education programs, due process, and parent resource centers.

PART III: BRINGING INCLUSION INTO THE CLASSROOM: TEACHING ISSUES

Chapter 9: Learning About Disabilities

Written Materials

Batshaw, M., & Perret, Y. (1992). *Children with disabilities: A medical primer* (3rd ed.). Baltimore: Paul H. Brookes Publishing Co. A textbook with descriptive information about disabilities and a helpful glossary.

Doggett, L., & George, J. (1993). *All kids count: Child care and the Americans with Disabilities Act.* Arlington, TX: The Arc National Headquarters. (Available from The Arc, Post Office Box 1047, Arlington, TX 76004; [817] 261-6003, [817] 277-0553 [TDD]). A very helpful guide about the ADA and serving children with special needs. The resource list is very comprehensive and has resources related to specific disabilities.

Agencies

The Council for Exceptional Children
ERIC Clearinghouse on Handicapped and Gifted Children
1920 Association Drive
Reston, VA 22091-1589
(703) 264-9494 (fax)

The ERIC Clearinghouse has fact sheets on individual disabilities. This information is in the public domain and can be reproduced.

National Information Center for Children
and Youth with Disabilities (NICHY)
Post Office Box 1492
Washington, D.C. 20013
1-800-999-5599

NICHY is a national information and referral clearinghouse. It provides free fact sheets on all major disability categories as well as information about additional sources of information.

Chapter 10: Talking About Disabilities

Written Materials

Chapel Hill Training-Outreach Project. (1983). *The new friends curriculum.* Chapel Hill, NC: Author. A training curriculum with specific topics, activities, and ideas for people interested in including children with special needs in early childhood programs.

Derman-Sparks, L., & A.B.C. Task Force. (1989). *The anti-bias curriculum.* Washington, DC: National Association for the Education of Young Children. (Available from National Association for the Education of Young Children, 1834 Connecticut Avenue, NW, Washington, D.C. 20009). A curriculum book for addressing many kinds of differences—gender, race, and abilities. Includes activities and resources.

Froschles, M., Colon, L., Rubin, E., & Sprung, B. (1984). *Including all of us: An early childhood curriculum about disability.* Mt. Ranier, MD: Gryphon House. A curriculum book that includes many ideas for activities to do with children.

Quinsey, M.B. (1986). *Why does that man have such a big nose?* Seattle, WA: Parenting Press. A book that depicts many of the hard questions young children ask their teachers and parents, and it includes answers that can be given.

Chapter 11: Classroom Strategies

Written Materials

Abraham, M.R., Morris, L., & Wald, P. (1993). *Inclusive early childhood education.* Tucson, AZ: Communication Skill Builders. This book describes the theory and practice of implementing a program that serves the individual needs of typically developing children as well as children with mild to moderate developmental delays.

Cronburg, J.G., Barnett, J., & Goldman, N. (1993). *Readily achievable checklist: A survey for accessibility.* Boston: Adaptive Environments Center. (Available from the American Occupational Therapy Association, 1383 Piccard Drive, Post Office Box 1725, Rockville, MD 20849-1725; [301] 948-9626, 1-800-377-8555 [TDD]; or Adaptive Environments Center, 374 Congress Street, Suite 301, Boston, MA 02210; [617] 695-1225 [voice/TDD]). This booklet contains a process to evaluate the accessibility of a facility.

The Great Lakes Resource Access Project. (1992–1993). *The Americans with Disabilities Act and Head Start: Practical strategies for developing compliance plans* [Quarterly Resource], *7*(1). (Available from Great Lakes Resource Access Project, University of Illinois, Department of Special Education, 403 East Healey, Champaign, IL 61820; [217] 333-3876).

Index

Page numbers followed by "f" indicate figures; those followed by "t" indicate tables.